CABLE TELEVISION AND THE FUTURE
OF BROADCASTING

CABLE TELEVISION
and the Future
of Broadcasting

Edited by RALPH M. NEGRINE

ST. MARTIN'S PRESS
New York

6.92

12313299

© 1985 Ralph M. Negrine
All rights reserved. For information, write:
St. Martin's Press, Inc., 175 Fifth Avenue, New York, NY 10010
Printed in Great Britain
First published in the United States of America in 1985

Library of Congress Cataloging in Publication Data
Main entry under title:
Cable television and the future of broadcasting.

    Includes bibliographies and index.
    1. Cable television—Addresses, essays, lectures.
I. Negrine, Ralph M.
HE8700.7.C33   1985   384.55'47   85-14582
ISBN 0-312-11318-8

CONTENTS

Contents

TABLES AND FIGURES

Tables

Figure

INTRODUCTION

Ralph Negrine

This book is intended to fulfil two main functions.
Firstly, to provide a general survey of developments in specific countries and, secondly, to give
the reader the opportunity to assess the promise of
cable television, to gauge its rate of development
and to measure its likely impact on existing
broadcasting services. In a rapidly changing
environment, such aims may appear over-ambitious
but there is sufficient common ground between
nations to make some important comparisons possible
and worthwile. Some of these comparisons, and
indeed the similarities, will be considered here.
    Cable television remains, after more than 30
years of development a distribution system. But
the nature of that distribution system has changed
quite dramatically over its relatively short
life-span: cable television systems today have an
enormously increased capacity and the more technologically advanced broadband cable systems can
even carry a variety of data and interactive
services. Such changes, in isolation, may not
appear significant but their combination within a
single wired network opens up a range of
possibilities for mass and inter-personal communication hitherto only dreamt of. The concept of 'The
Wired Nation'[1] which refers to a society wherein a
wide range of services - both telecommunications
and entertainment - are supplied to all through a
national network of (optical fibre) cables is
therefore not too far-fetched, as the French
attempt to construct this society illustrates. More
problematic though, as the chapters in this book
point out, is how to reach that goal.
    It has not always been the potential for
greater telecommunication that has made cable
television so central an issue in the last two

1

decades. Admittedly, governments have often stated their desires to achieve the goal of the wired society but, in practice, it remains the case that it is the public's real desire for more television entertainment services - and entrepreneurial incentive to satisfy this desire - that has propelled cable from a secondary and supplementary distribution system to a potentially prime one. Herein lies one of the major contradictions in the development of cable systems: are cable systems essentially entertainment systems or are they primarily telecommunications systems which can also carry entertainment services? Furthermore, what is the present relationship between these two features of cable and what should that relationship be in the future and as the technology becomes even more sophisticated? Finally, should cable systems be regulated as public utilities or should they be allowed to function as private enterprises seeking profits and expansion?

There are many answers to these questions and each individual country has its own preferences. Nonetheless, these preferences are made known within a certain context: a realisation that cable systems will develop only as a response to the pressure for more entertainment services over, and above, that which already exists. This factor is fairly common across all the countries surveyed here and goes some way towards explaining why the issue of cable has moved to the centre of media debates in the last ten years.

In that period, cable's fortunes were transformed. This transformation, which happened in the mid 1970s, was the result of changes in two areas. Firstly, the means to deliver more, and different, services were developed and proved to be, in the main, profitable. Secondly, decisions were taken which permitted both cable's physical expansion and its fuller exploitation.

These two changes took place at different times in different countries. The US was the first country to experience the full array of services that broadcasting by satellite to cable systems made possible. Home Box Office (HBO) is perhaps the most successful of these services to date and it does demonstrate the ways in which these services can break out of the traditional pattern of television broadcasting. They eschew the general, the Lowest Common Denominator type of programmes and direct their material to specific audiences -the young, the film fan, the sports fan and so on.

2

The popularity of these services was assured once the link with cable systems was complete and the regulatory frameworks surrounding cable systems were measurably relaxed. An audience could then easily be reached without recourse to the expensive and more powerful Direct Broadcasting by Satellite (DBS) system of distribution. Moreover, the public did not have to purchase a dish aerial for the reception of these services. Satellite broadcasting, with the aid of cable systems, effectively created new, and sometimes better, national networks - Home Box Office, Cable News Network and so on.

This growth in services in the US was soon to have both a real physical effect, and a psychological impact, on Europe. It made Europeans - and their governments - aware of possible new areas for technological expansion and growth and, more critically, it made them aware of impending changes. Europe would no longer be able to keep the satellite services (or their backers) out: governments would have to devise ways and means to soften their impact. The 'para-national' corporations predicted by Raymond Williams ten years ago[2] were, therefore instrumental in making Europe aware of the potential of the new technologies. The British Information Technology Advisory Panel (see p. 111) was, for example, much influenced by the American experience.

Individual governments outside the US have responded in different ways to the promise of cable television and satellite broadcasting. Those with significant cable systems, for example, Canada and the Low Countries, have attempted to combine continued growth with a measure of protection for their indigenous cultural needs and services. Hence the complex set of frameworks and regulations that apply in each of these countries. It is, however, the other major European states - Germany, Britain, France - that have highlighted the crucial issues surrounding cable television in the 1980s and beyond. Because these nations have neither significant cable systems nor satellite broadcasting services of their own, they were not restricted to a narrow and well-defined range of policy options for the future. In fact, they have all had to make crucial decisions on the future of cable systems and networks and the relationship between entertainment and telecommunications services on such systems and networks.

For these nations, the policy options were

3

complicated by other considerations. Namely, the realisation that the technologies in question were somehow inter-related (converging) and so could not be treated separately. Furthermore, each country felt it needed to make a definite commitment to the new technologies if it wished to encourage, and protect, its respective industrial sectors. As Howkins has written:

> The convergence of signals (e.g. videotex, electronic mail, subscription TV) is blurring the regulatory and cultural characteristics of each category. Not only are the devices complementary (e.g. cable, satellites) but also the services (e.g. news bulletins, tele-text) and functions (e.g. multi-channel, time-shifting). Changes in one will often influence others ....The greatest pressure for change comes from the imaginative use of cable and the encouragement of private competition in telecommunications...[3]

The result of this new emphasis on the information technologies was to transform yester-years's cable television into tomorrow's broadband cable systems. But, as indicated above, the problem remained of how to make the transition from one to the other: for example, co-axial or optical fibre cables, tree and branch or star-switched, imported technology or indigenous technology, gradual expansion or all-out growth. As the 'no change' option seemed no longer available to any of these countries, it became a matter of choosing the most suitable and appropriate set of policies for achieving their desired goals. In all cases, though, each of the policy options had widespread consequences of an economic, political, social and cultural kind.

Whilst each country considered these options, there was common agreement on two points. Firstly, that the telecommunications side of cable systems was some way off in the future and depended on the prior existence of a broadband cable system; secondly, that the public's desire for entertain-ment services was more certain than its desire for other communications facilities. In fact, it had had very little experience of the latter. The issue was how to combine this knowledge with the objective of the wired society. It is worth contrasting the French and British approach as an illustration of the complexity of the issue.

France has put forward a long-term strategy for the cabling of its population and that policy also makes provisions for a variety of telecommunications services. This policy grants the state a major role in funding and directing the development of cable systems though it does offer a degree of autonomy to local (private and public) initiatives in relation to the construction and marketing of such systems. It is envisaged that, ultimately, both entertainment and telecommunications will be part and parcel of this major development programme.

In contrast, the British Conservative government has been unwilling to play an active part in the development of cable systems in Britain. Instead, all cable developments will be privately funded and future developments will be based on the entertainment-led policy, that is, public demand for entertainment cable will finance and so pull through the more long term benefits of broadband cable. Other countries examined in this book illustrate the available range of options which appear to fall between these two extremes.

That there are major weaknesses in both approaches should come as no surprise. The danger in both cases is that these weaknesses may be so severe that the final goal of 'the wired nation' may itself be at stake. In the case of the French Plan Cable, Bertrand rightly asks whether it is anything more than yet another (unattainable) French 'grand plan'. Will it be another Concorde? Where will the funds come from? Such questions do not arise in the same way in the case of Britain for the approach here has been more circumspect and the costs and benefits of success (or failure) will be borne directly and solely by the private entrepreneur. The state has effectively delegated all responsibility to the private sector even though it provides the major regulatory framework for cable.

But broadband cable systems are a high risk, capital intensive industry. In Britain, cable operators have not found it easy to make friends and allies of institutional investors and this has had an impact on the rate of development. It is not that cable's future as an entertainment medium is in doubt - whether in 'pilot projects' or 'upgraded systems' (pp. 117) - but its long term future as part of a national broadband communications network may be far more difficult to finance. It seems likely that for broadband cable systems to exist nationally, or even to pass about 50 per cent of all British households, both government funding and an even greater liberalisation of the technical and content regulations currently in force are necessary. In other words, the economics of cable in the free-market may militate against the more futuristic aspects of contemporary developments.

There are then some inherent contradictions in British policy; but these contradictions cannot be resolved within the framework of a policy that aims to please a government with a non-interventionist philosophy of encouraging private enterprise. That some of Britain's future broadband cable operators have been pleading and lobbying the government for both financial and regulatory changes is a clear indication of their dilemmas.

Though this particular situation is unique to Britain, it does illustrate in a general way the sorts of obstacles that can lie in the path of the process of cabling a nation. And those obstacles have consequences both in the short term, for example, will the nation ever be cabled at all, and in the long term, for example, if cabled, what sort of system will a nation acquire?

The last two countries reviewed in this book - Australia and Japan - offer extreme examples of what cable technology signifies. In the Australian context, cable television has been examined, assessed and finally relegated in view of the growing popularity of VCRs. As Caldwell notes, the need for more home-based entertainment can be easily satisfied through the 'alternative' technology of VCRs rather than the more costly and long-term development of cable systems. In this respect, there are parallels between the Australian case and some European examples such as Britain, where the two systems may be in direct competition for the viewers.

In contrast, Japan has pursued the development of cable systems within the framework of its national telecommunications policy. This is, in itself, a departure from the other countries reviewed here. It is, however, within this context that we have to understand and analyse the role of cable technology in Japan. As Tracey points out, from the British, and perhaps the European perspective, the tone of the Japanese debate is quite different and there is a lack of interest in cable as a source of more entertainment. What interests the Japanese then is not more television qua entertainment but cable systems as part and parcel of the development towards the production and distribution of information.

In reviewing the chapters in this book, one becomes aware of at least three other concerns. These are as follows:

1. <u>The impact on existing broadcasting organisations</u> In the more immediate future, the recurrent problem for most of the countries examined here is the nature of the co-existence between entertainment cable and the various existing broadcasting institutions, in particular those founded on public service principles. The most popular resolution of this problem is the creation of the 'must carry' rule which ensures that all national broadcasting services continue to be made available to all. This decision typifies the common concern felt about cable's challenge to, and impact on, broadcasting services. By guaranteeing broadcasting a place on the cable menu, it is felt that a measure of protection is afforded.

But this solution can be both short-sighted and, in its way, unsatisfactory. It is short-sighted if it misinterprets the nature of cable's challenge. As the Pilkington Committee remarked after its investigation of pay-TV in 1960:

> ...the method of financing broadcasting is not a matter of indifference, not merely a means to an end. It is of constitutional significance because it affects the end; that is because it affects the nature and character of the service provided. Further, if two or more services are competing, the nature and character of one is likely to affect those of the others. As a method of payment, subscription must be judged, therefore, not only by its effect on the character of the service it is meant to pay for, but also by its effect upon existing services to the public.[4]

It may also be unsatisfactory if it does not ensure that the aims and objectives of the existing broadcasting institutions continue to be represented in the new competitive media environment. It should be recalled that many of the European institutions are of a public service character and display a variety of mechanisms by which a country's social and political structures are presented. These arrangements include the public authority structure of British broadcasting, the representative council of the Rundfunkrat, the less widely representative

7

though politically accountable French structure,
the Dutch religious and political balances, the
Belgian language divide and so on. There are, it is
clear, major internal differences which make each
of these systems unique but nevertheless the
chapters in this book suggest that these structures
are characteristic of attempts to prevent broadcasting - an all important medium of mass communication - from becoming no more than a low quality
entertainment medium.

Yet few countries have attempted to go beyond
the 'must carry' rules so as to ensure that some
continuity will exist with the traditions of
accountability and responsibility. The Germans
insistence on representative control boards is
perhaps the major exception here though there are
grave doubts about the coherence of the legislation.

In all the other cases, direct competition
between the existing broadcasting services and
cable TV has been allowed despite the concern of
many that the final result may be disadvantageous
to the nature of public service broadcasting and to
the consumer. It is too early to pass judgement on
this issue. It has been said that cable television
in the US has provided a welcome change from the
established media institutions and forced them to
adapt for the better. But because European broadcasting systems are different from those of the US,
one should not necessarily expect the same
beneficial outcomes. European systems appear to
have a great deal more to lose. Whether this will
turn out to be the case is a matter for future
social scientists to judge.

A common feature of most of the cable systems
reviewed in this text is that they are mainly
private enterprises operating within a regulatory
framework provided by their respective states. This
is also a feature of sytems where there is an
element of both state funding and state control, as
in France. These enterprises are required to comply
with certain minimal rules. Typically, these rules
set out what entertainment services cable systems
may carry and in what priority, for example, 'must
carry', DBS, local services, access services and so
on. In addition, there are usually regulations
concerning advertising, adult channels, religious
services, news services and the like. In practice,
the differences between countries are immense and
they reflect political, social and economic
ideologies. All these approaches are dealt with, in
detail, in the chapters below.

There is, however, one point that emerges in the chapter on the US experience which is not explicitly dealt with elsewhere. It seems clear that the US has been concerned with the nature of cable television to a far greater extent than other countries. There are questions raised - in academic, public and legal circles - about whether cable is a common carrier or not; whether cable is more like publishing than broadcasting and whether regulations should, or could, cover these elements. This concern may be due to the nature of competition in the US and the recourse to law. These aspects of cable TV have been fairly peripheral to the European debate and this has had a tendency to allow for a continuity of policy so minimising the extent to which official positions and decisions are questioned.

2. Community and access channels Within this array of rules and prohibitions one can also find recommendations for local and community access channels or programmes. Again the details vary from country to country but the underlying philosophy is remarkably similar across all states. As a reaction against mediated, depersonalised and mass communication, access and community programmes (or channels) are meant to reflect the real desires and needs of local communities.

In the late 1960s and early 1970s, such services were synonymous with cable television's potential for radical change in the field of broadcasting. Experimental services sprang up across Europe and North America and individuals and communities found, for the first time, an opportunity to make their own programmes. This led, in turn, to a process whereby the medium of television lost its mysterious and distant qualities and was within reach of everyone.

Few of the European experiments have survived into the 1980s though they continue to exist elsewhere. Their difficulties have always been economic. Communities or localities rarely feel that they can afford such luxuries and the emphasis has usually been on the cable operator to provide both studio facilities and technical equipment. As the 'returns' on this investment - in terms of interest or increased subscriber connections - have never been sufficient to justify continued expenditure, the experiments, certainly the European ones, have always led a precarious existence. But the evidence cited in this book suggests that regulators and even some cable

operators see community type channels as both a
necessary and desirable part of what is, typically,
a local cable operation. Such views, however, do
not make much impact on the fundamental weakness of
such services: who wil fund them? What are the
cable operators precise obligations towards
community type channels? Who decides whether they
are viable or not? What sorts of criteria -
financial, social, political - will be used to
judge the success and long term viability of these
services?

These questions indicate a general concern
over the future - as opposed to the desirability -
of these services. Cable systems can enhance
communications on the local level but will the
issue of economic profitability intrude to such an
extent as to diminish the likelihood of such
services being offered? The next few years will
provide us with the necessary information on which
to judge the future of such channels.

3. The new media's impact on cultures There
is little doubt that satellite broadcasting and
cable television will have consequences which will
gradually be felt right across Europe. Slowly, but
surely, satellite broadcasting will unite these
countries into a large media market. Whether the
service provides entertainment (Sky Channel), films
or the arts, the effect is to over-ride national
boundaries. The French have indicated their concern
and others, notably Germany, have expressed theirs.
Their fears for their cultures and production
facilities are real fears and reflect widespread
concern over impending changes. But it is too early
to say if the pressure of competition from imports
(cheap or otherwise) will affect the quality, and
the range, of the work of the existing broadcasting
institutions.

Such fears may be exaggerated; if cable is no
more than a minority medium then its impact may be
very limited. But there is a real danger that in
the new competitive media environment attempts to
retain or increase ones share of the finite
audience will result in the erosion of the quality
of content.

These fears, and the policy options discussed
above, form the backdrop to this book. There are
many challenges that have to be confronted if the
'wired nation' is to remain more than a forlorn
hope. But in pressing for action, one also needs
to pay attention to the nature of, and the rationale

behind, the development of the new technologies. A decade ago, Raymond Williams wrote that 'the new technology is itself a product of a particular social system, and will be developed as an apparently autonomous process of innovation only to the extent that we fail to identify and challenge its real agencies.' It was, he continued, 'a process of development which was full of contradictions because the new technologies could be used in many ways, and even for purposes, which differed from those of the existing social order.' He concluded that 'the choices and uses ... made will in any case be part of a more general process of social development, social growth and social struggle.'[5]

Critical reviews of the new information technologies have gone even further in their emphasis on the (almost hidden) nature of technological development. As Robins and Webster have argued:

> information technology has been _shaped_ by multinational corporations ... to express specific corporate values and priorities. There is no reason to believe that it will not reinforce, and aggravate, existing inequalities at both the national and international levels.[6]

These statements provide a much needed corrective to the optimistic forecasts of 'the wired nation' since they make us aware that technological developments take place within a certain configuration of social, political and economic factors. Development is not autonomous and although the public may have an opportunity to direct the nature of that development, the process of 'social struggle' is one in which the public plays a small part. For example, in none of the countries reviewed here has there been a lengthy period of public consultation on the future of cable systems. Furthermore, cable systems have been designed to exploit certain aspects of industrial development. Security systems, tele-shopping, tele-banking, data processing and the like are, if anything, sophisticated ways of restructuring labour processes in a range of marketing, banking and office systems. Rarely have cable systems been designed and developed as means of enhancing community communications. Entertainment cable may be no more than a sophisticated and carefully packaged and presented shopping arcade to numb the television viewer.

It is obvious that cable systems (and satellite broadcasting) touch many areas of life which had been previously isolated and secure from radical change. The electronics industries have promised the public a new world, a new infrastructure for the last decade of this century, but how many of these changes will actually come about is a matter for debate. The chapters in this book suggest that the entertainment cable revolution may shortly be upon us. As cable and satellite services fight for survival with the proliferation of Video Cassette Recorders (VCR), the range of material available will surely expand. But it is, for some, a hard struggle. The Australian experience, now matched by the American one, suggests that there may be a direct conflict between the popularity and flexibility of VCRs and the capital intensive, high risk features of cable systems. Such a conflict may, in the short run, be to the disadvantage of cable. Similarly, competition between cable and satellite transmissions may also be to the disadvantage of the former.

The authors included here are generally more circumspect about the other facilities - the value added services - that are so central to the broadband cable revolution. The famous American advanced interactive services have after all found it too costly to continue to operate and have pulled back from the more futuristic services that they had initially promised. If this situation is replicated elsewhere, then cable's future as an interactive communication network may remain only a 'pipe dream'.

In the near future, it is almost certain that many of us in urban districts will have access to a growing menu of entertainment television. We will be able to focus on our favourite material without having to suffer unwanted interruptions (in the form of advertisements) or diversions (in the form of news and current affairs material). In time, our television sets <u>may</u> also provide us with the opportunity to bank and shop from home. Though these latter services will clearly depend on the service provider's willingness to organise, fund and market such a service and a more thorough assessment - as opposed to optimistic predictions - of public demand.

In other words, what the converging technologies <u>can do</u> and <u>will do</u> will depend on the economic viability of the array of entertainment and other services that are dangled, carrot-like, in front of us. In this way, cable systems merely create a complex series of commodity markets - information, entertainment - in which we, the consumers, must participate.

Finally, a brief description of this book. It is not technical and though it does make references to different cable systems and configurations, for example, fibre-optic as against co-axial cable, they are usually presented as alternative policy options which different states have to decide upon. For this reason, the reader will not find technical discussions about the options available. The aim of this book is to highlight a central theme, that is, the challenge of cable television to broadcasting and telecommunications in the 1980s and beyond.

A book such as this inevitably risks being out of date before publication. In dealing with rapidly changing social, political and technical environments it is difficult to predict detailed changes. As a result, it is possible that some of the details, for example relating to individual companies or particular company plans, will be out of date. Similarly, as the industry world wide goes through changes and meets different challenges, it is possible that optimism rapidly turns to pessimism. Such changes are notorious and have plagued the cable industry over the last 30 or so years. This should not, one hopes, weaken the overall arguments presented in each chapter since these are more concerned with the general processes and economic, social and technical forces that will dictate the future of cable television. It is therefore hoped that the issues raised here will remain of interest for years to come.

NOTES

1 R.L.Smith,(1972), The Wired Nation.
2 R.Williams, (1974), Television:Technology and Cultural Form, Fontana, London, p.138.
3 J.Howkins, (1982), New Technologies, New Policies? BFI, London, pp. 1-2.
4 Report of the Committee on Broadcasting, 1960, (1962), Cmnd 1753, HMSO, London, paragraph 972.
5 R.Williams, (1974), Television:Technology and Cultural Form, pp. 135-136.
6 K.Robins and F.Webster, (1983), Information Technology, Luddism and the Working Class, in V.Mosco and J.Wasko, (eds.) (1983), The Critical

Introduction

Communications Review, Volume One, _The Working Class and the Media_. Ablex, New Jersey, p. 202. Emphasis supplied.

Chapter One

CABLE TELEVISION IN THE UNITED STATES: A STORY OF
CONTINUING GROWTH AND CHANGE

Vernone Sparkes

By the end of 1985, at least 45 and possibly 50 per
cent of US television households will be receiving
some type of cable television service. By the end
of the decade, with the final wiring of the
remaining large cities, penetration can be expected
to move up towards 62-65 per cent, where, unless
there are any major government or industry policy
changes, penetration growth will likely level off,
with only gradual increase thereafter, upwards to
the 70 per cent range. While consumer reticence and
competition from other telecommunications technologies
together point to such a growth plateau, majority
opinion is still that cable television, or at least
some type of broadband 'wire' distribution system,
will be the dominant telecommunications transmission
system in the United States for the next several
decades.
     Not a few observers of this emerging
technology have hailed what they perceive to be the
'revolution' inherent in cable television.[1] While
current realities have not matched some of the more
exotic expectations, broad impact is clearly
involved. Indeed, the history of the medium, and
the industries that have developed along with it,
has always been characterised by surprising change:
change in industry structure, change in public
policy, and change in consumer attitude. Thus while
the thesis of 'revolution' might be applied at best
with some hesitation to the development of cable
television in the United States, the theme of
evolution is certainly most appropriate.
     The complexity of this evolution, both past
and projected, will strike those used to a more
centralised approach to telecommunications policy
as close to chaotic. For one thing, it is an
evolution marked by paradoxes. Cable television can

be simultaneously hailed as the means of greatly
increased content diversity, and of greatly
increased content control. It is viewed as both a
tool for increased democratisation of American
society and as the weapon of ultimate totalitarianism.
It is argued to provide new opportunity for greater
humanisation of the society, and of foreshadowing a
depersonalisation and fragmentation of the society.

Also, it is an evolution involving many
different players and constantly shifting alliances.
When specifically speaking of 'Cable Television' in
the US context, one is pointing to a particular
business arrangement and set of telecommunications
services. But while the Cable Television industry
is presently the dominant actor in the arena of new
telecommunications technologies, it's prominance is
hardly assured. There are other technologies in the
wings - Direct Broadcast Satellite, MDS, VCR, LPTV.
Thus in monitoring the US scene one must
differentiate between current organisations and the
broader telecommunications field. New interactive
services which might fail with the cable television
industry could still find viability through new
telephone industry technology, for example.
Videotex is considered one of the more natural
adjuncts to cable television, and yet public
diffusion of videotex service might be most
dependent upon the spread of home computers.

At the present time, however, there is a
discrete combination of technologies, institutions,
and people we can call the cable television
industry, and it is the development and future of
this industry in the United States that this essay
seeks to explicate.

To provide a basic context for the discussion
which follows, a summarisation of cable television
in the United States today would seem appropriate
at the outset.

1. The industry began in 1948, and today
   features close to 6000 individual systems,
   with a combined total of over 35 million
   subscribers. It is presently growing at a
   rate of almost one half million subscribers
   a month.
2. These systems, with some very minor
   exceptions, are privately owned, and
   operated for profit from retailing programming
   services from a wide variety of sources.
3. Cable television in the United States is
   regulated on the local, state and federal

    levels of government, with jurisdictional
    lines a matter of dispute. The basic
    operating licence, or franchise, is
    granted by the local city government.
4. Subscriber fees range from two to five
    dollars for a simple twelve channel
    service, to 10-15 dollars for thirty six
    to fifty-four channel 'converter service'.
    Special pay channels can then be added at
    an average rate of 10 dollars each.
    Installation is either free, or in the $25
    range.

IN THE BEGINNING THERE WAS LOCALISM

Effort towards national or centralised planning of
communications in the United States are commonly
considered contrary to the diversity objectives of
the First Amendment of the US constitution, and
inappropriate to the very size of the country
itself. So it is appropriate that the single most
influential idea in the early days of cable
development was that of local television service.[2]
The notion that broadcast stations were essentially
to be local media lay at the heart of the US Radio
Act of 1927, and subsequently the 1934 Communications Act. The fact that national networks so
quickly came to dominate first radio and then
television certainly bothered federal authorities,
but they never were able to do much about it.
Indeed, moving from the 1941 Networking Rules,[3]
through the ill-fated Blue Book,[4] to the 1960
Programming Policy Statement,[5] one witnesses a
gradual but steady pragmatic retreat by the Federal
Communications Commission (FCC) from this local
service objective.[6]
    Nevertheless, the ideology of local service
ran deep. It was because of this concern that in
1948 the FCC called a halt to television station
licensing. They had decided it was necessary to
rework the national television spectrum allocation
plan to provide for more local television stations
in US communities. There are two points about this
'freeze' which were important to the development of
cable television. The first was short term. The
freeze meant that many communities which had
anxiously awaited the arrival of television service
now had to wait a little longer.
    Retailers of television receiving sets in
these communities found themselves with stores full
of television sets no one wanted to buy, so some
enterprising merchants took matters into their own
hands. The idea was to find a good location, erect

a 'Community Antenna', run some wires to interested customers, and at last sell those receivers. The cable television industry had begun.

Broadcasters and government alike fully expected this phenomenon to disappear with the final lifting in 1952 of the television freeze. And so it might have, had it not been for another aspect of the local service philosophy. In seeking to maximise the number of communities with their own local television station, interference was a major problem, so the FCC had to limit the number of stations assigned to each community. Thus, instead of a large region having, say, six different stations serving everyone in the area, the six frequencies were divided among the local cities, with only 2-3 televisiion stations available in any given community. The frequency allocation plan devised to assure localism, then, resulted in an artificial limit on the number of television stations in individual US communities. So where cable television proved useful for bringing television service to communities that had no station at all, it also served to increase the number of stations available in other communities, even large cities like San Diego. In retrospect, then, it is not surprising that cable television continued to grow after the lifting of the television licence freeze in 1952.

Broadcasters, who had initially welcomed the new medium as a means of extending their markets, now feared that the technology was having the reverse effect. Signals brought in from other cities were thought to draw audience away from the local stations. The implications for advertising revenue naturally concerned the local broadcasters, and the National Association of Broadcasters (NAB) was accordingly not long in seeking relief from the federal government.

Such protestations initially fell on deaf ears in both Congress and at the FCC. Finally responding to NAB complaints, in 1959 the FCC considered the matter, but decided that cable television fell outside of their jurisdictional mandate. Congress came close to enacting legislation, but the action died due to a general lack of interest. In the meantime, the cable television industry, now employing microwave transmission to move broadcast signals around the country, continued to grow.

By the early 1960s, however, things began to stir in Washington. What stimulated this activity was again the local service preoccupation. Simply

put, the FCC finally became aware of the
possibility that the spread of cable television
could undermine the entire television broadcast
structure. Fragmentation of local audiences could
well decrease resources for local programme
production, and that, believed the Commission,
could not be allowed to happen. After several
hesitant steps to exercise authority over the new
industry, in 1966 the Commission completely
reversed its earlier hands-off stance and declared
total jurisdiction, calling a halt to distant
signal importation into the nation's top 100
markets.[7] The theretofore rapid growth of cable
television slowed precipitously, and what was to be
a long struggle over jurisdiction and objectives
for this new technology began.

    The irony of this early period, of course, is
that the FCC was caught in the position of
retarding a technology with tremendous local
service potential, for the sake of protecting a
technology that for all practical purposes had
become a three-way national monopoly.

A NEW INDUSTRY TAKES SHAPE

The development of what we call 'Cable Television'
has been characterised by three phases. In the late
1940s and through the 1950s, the primary technological
feature of these systems was indeed the large
antenna erected to pick up such broadcast signals
as might be available in the area. These early
systems were truly Community Antenna Television, or
CATV. Most of those early systems were 12 channels
or less and were established in small communities,
usually beyond effective home reception range of
broadcast television stations. Several thousand
such systems, with their emphasis on retransmission
of broadcast signals, survive today. Recent
estimates are that they still comprise 70 per cent
of the total systems in the United States, although
they serve less than 35 per cent of all
subscribers.

    With improvements in technology and an
interest in establishing cable systems in larger
cities, particularly ones with some local television
service already, the emphasis shifted away from the
master antenna and towards the use of microwave for
the importation of increasingly distant broadcast
signals.

    As previously noted, the number of broadcast
television channels available to most communities

is three or fewer, with each station affiliated
with one of the three commercial television
networks. With this national affiliation pattern,
television service across the nation was very
homogeneous. True differences in available
television service came down to the number of
independent stations (i.e. not affiliated with any
of the networks) a community had. It was these
independent television stations, then, that became
the basis of growth for the cable industry in
markets which already had network television
service.

During this phase, roughly corresponding to
the early 1970s, the concept of the 'super station'
emerged, as broadcast stations like WGN in Chicago
and WOR in New York were microwaved up to three
hundred miles to cable systems. With this change in
technological emphasis it now became more appropriate
to speak of 'Cable Television', rather than 'CATV'
as the attention was now on the capacity of this
co-axial technology to provide a large number of
channels to a community, channels that could
accommodate much more than a few local broadcast
stations. This shift in emphasis and operation
became even more pronounced with subsequent
development of programming services intended
specifically for cable television systems. Now
began the period of first 20 channel then 36
channel cable television systems, with the first
experiments in two-way services.

Some would argue that this second phase will
continue for some time, others that it is in the
process of ending already. The most critical point,
however, is not so much to pinpoint transition
times as to understand the nature of the change
involved. The change from the 'CATV' period to the
'Cable Television' period was characterised by an
expansion in the diversity and amount of television
programming. In this third phase, sometimes
referred to as the period of Broadband Telecommunications, attention moves beyond television
programming to a broad range of electronic
information services that can be accomodated on
this technology.

If precise dating of this shift is difficult,
it is fair to say it was with the beginning of the
1980s that true broadband telecommunications
systems became the norm for newly constructed
systems. Not surprisingly, this is also the period
when the largest American cities became the targets
of intense licence competition, as cable companies

vied for this remaining all important segment of
the US market. This is the period of the 50-100
channel system, with fully active two-way capacity,
computer assisted services and dedicated institutional
trunks. In addition to traditional television
programming, these systems are offering or are
capable of offering such services as videotex,
security alarm service, electronic shopping,
electronic mail service, and increasingly individual-
ised subscriber programming. As shall be discussed
at greater length below, however, it is not at all
clear at this point in time whether this third
phase defines the future for the cable television
industry, or signals the beginning of a much more
complex technological scenario in which cable
television will be but one participating industry,
even a transitional industry heralding the
emergence of fibre optic common carriers and
broadband DBS service.

Surprising as it might at first seem, members
of the cable television industry are not unanimous
on the matter of exactly what business they are
engaged in. To digress for a moment, it is helpful
to remember that the commercial broadcaster is in
the business of selling audiences to advertisers.
The movie theatre operator is in the business of
selling an entertainment feature to the consumer
public. A common carrier, on the other hand, is in
the business of selling a transmission service to
both audience and information suppliers. What is
the cable television operator of the early 1980s
selling?

Initially, he was most akin to the common
carrier operator, selling a transmission service.
With the development of first superstations, and
then pay television service, the cable operator
took on the business characteristics of the movie
theatre operator. With the emergence of advertising
on cable television, the cable operator shares with
the broadcaster the objective of selling audiences.
Finally, with provision of leased channels and
enhanced data transmission service the cable
operator again takes on the character of a common
carrier. This mixed model makes it difficult to
both manage a cable business and to analyse
industry economics. Predicting the financial health
of the medium involves much more than measuring the
limits of subscription fees.

The revenue realised by an 'average' cable
system in the United States in the 1980s is
primarily from service charges and programming fees

(Pay Cable directly, but indirectly for satellite delivered cable programming services as well). Income from cable advertising in the 1984 period reached 500 million dollars, with one billion projected for the immediate future.[8] Most of this goes directly to the national programming services at the present, but local operators (local systems) already generate $70 million in local advertising sales, and this figure too is expected to rise sharply.

— With income per subscriber presently averaging out around 25 dollars a month, the cable industry is hopeful that advertising income will continue to grow, providing needed revenues at a time of intense media competition. Finally, how much of the available media advertising dollars will shift to cable television remains to be seen. Some major advertising firms are advocating a much larger share for cable then is presently the case. The increasing availability of audience data is certainly helping. For the near future, however, subscriber fees will continue to be the primary source of income for the industry, and so development of programming the public will 'buy' will continue to be critical.

The cable industry then has gone through considerable change with regards to the nature of the programme services being sold to the public. Shifting first from local signals to distant broadcast signals, the industry is now more characterised by special cable programming services than it is by the retransmission of broadcast television signals. This is particularly true if one considers 'super stations' such as Ted Turner's WTBS as in reality a cable service more than a broadcast station.

The process by which this programming change has come about can be considered anything but orderly. As previously noted, the FCC moved in 1966 to place restrictions on cable importation of broadcast signals. The rules promulgated by the FCC at this time were actually intended to be a stop-gap measure, as it was fully anticipated that the courts would soon rule that unauthorised cable transmission of broadcast signals was an infringement of copyright. It was believed that once cable operators had to pay copyright fees for these signals, the industry would go out of business. The FCC, and the industry itself were surprised when in 1968 the Supreme Court ruled that the act of retransmitting broadcast signals was not a violation of copyright, and that the cable operators undertaking such a service were not liable for payment for these signals.[9]

It was because of this surprise ruling that the FCC finally got down to work on a comprehensive rulemaking for cable television. The results of this effort, published in 1972, involved a complex formula for cable carriage of distant broadcast signals, all presupposing lack of copyright obligations.[10] While somewhat restrictive, the formula was nevertheless sufficiently generous to the cable business to restimulate industry expansion. In promulgating these rules, the FCC appeared to abandon it's 'anti-CATV' stance in favour of a position that allowed for media competition.

In the meantime, the US Congress had been working on a new copyright act in which the new technologies of cable television and electronic copiers were specifically addressed. With passage of this new act in 1976, cable operators for the first time became liable for copyright payment.[11] Administration and review of the payment terms were to be handled by a newly created commission called the Copyright Royalty Tribunal. The initial fees worked out were minimal, and in conjunction with the FCC's formula for carriage of distant broadcast signals seemed to provide a fair solution.

The FCC, however, subsequently determined that the passage of a new copyright act obviated the need for complex rules on signal carriage, and so dropped their carriage restrictions in 1980. Suddenly cable operators found themselves with no regulatory restrictions and minimal copyright fees. It seemed too good to be true, and in fact the situation did not last long. In response to the change in FCC rules, the Copyright Tribunal reformulated the fees, requiring cable operators to pay a substantial amount for any new signals added after the elimination of the FCC restrictions. This fee increase effectively reestablished the original 1972 FCC formula as the determining rule. Cable interests have since tried repeatedly to persuade Congress to intervene and roll back the Tribunal's rates, but this does not seem a likely prospect. So as of 1984 cable operators are economically restricted to 2-3 distant television signals (depending on the size of the market). If they wish to expand their programming offerings beyond that they have two choices; spend a fair amount of money for other distant signals (such could cost the operator around $300,000 in a city of 200,000 people) or add cable programming services. This forced choice has definitely helped some newer satellite services which otherwise were having a difficult time persuading system operators to carry them.

If regulation has been an impetus to the development of cable programming services, the emergence of satellites as a means of national distribution was the key facilitating factor. Home Box Office was the first service to take advantage of the satellite, making a bold move in 1975 to acquire a transponder for such purposes. By 1984, HBO had gone from a small regional service to a nationally distributed service of 13 million subscribers. The age of satellite interconnection of cable systems had arrived.

From the beginning, cable had been touted as the medium of the specialised programme, or narrowcasting. However, not surprisingly the first cable programming services were clearly designed with the mass audience in mind. Indeed, this was true both for the pay services with their emphasis on popular movies, and other early services which balanced off-network materials with sports. It was not until the early 1980s that services even approaching narrowcasting arrived on the scene. With the development of such specialised services as the Arts and Entertainment Channel, Lifetime, Music Television, Cable News Network , and a host of ethnic channels, specialisation was well underway.

Cable television has also brought about a promising expansion of international programming. While Public Broadcasting has long offered a modest diet of British television, the Arts and Entertainment Channel has greatly expanded the selection. The Spanish International Network provides Mexican and Spanish programming, while the Satellite Program Network presents specially prepared materials from Japan, Israel, Scandinavia and the Netherlands. Even the mass audience Entertainment and sports Network (ESPN) offers Canadian football and 'Soccer: Made In Germany'.

At the present time it is far too early to project which or how many of these new, specialised programming services will survive. Several services, including efforts by broadcast giants CBS and Westinghouse have already had to shut down, after spending millions in development capital. Others are facing several years more of struggle to make the break-even point. But clearly there are more than a few production and programming groups who believe cable television does offer a viable outlet for new programming, and that there is audience out there to support such. Some of this support will come by way of highly targeted advertising, some by way of special subscriber fees. Different economic arrangements will be tried as programmers look for the best financial model for their particular 'product'. By mid 1984, there were 36 such national programming ventures underway.

There is some belief that all but three to four of these new services will end in failure because, it is contended, the three large broadcasting networks are already providing enough of what the viewers 'really' want. Further support for this prediction is drawn from studies that show viewers seldom use more than 5-6 channels, no matter how many are available.[12] On the other side, however, is data indicating that the network share of audience drops to the 50 per cent range among households with full cable service.[13] Other information indicates that while viewers might settle on 5-6 channels, it is going to be a different set of 5 for each viewer. So the 36 or 54 channels of a modern cable system are still important for the satisfaction of this varied subscriber interest.

Still, many questions remain concerning the development of programming for cable television in the US. What new programming ideas will viewers support and what not? Even lacking support in the short run, will some new types of programming in fact develop viewer interest over time, as public expectations about television programming change? Also, what financial arrangements will work best for what kinds of programming and how much advertising money and consumer spending can be expected? Certainly the market place is adjusting. Few people 20 years ago would have believed that someday television viewers would pay an average of 25 dollars a month for cable service when broadcast television was available to them free.

A word needs to be said about a form of programming that is just now developing in the US market, but which some believe will be a critically important part of cable service in the future - pay-per-view (PPV). While the idea of a customer paying for only those programmes actually watched is almost as old as pay television itself, it has not been until very recently that the technology to efficiently provide this kind of service has been available. Curiously the technology did not develop with PPV in mind, but rather to combat signal piracy. The addressable converter helps do this by providing the system operator with centralised control over which signals go into each home. Computer controlled switching allows channels to be turned on or off almost instantly in contrast to the delays and logistics required when a technician had to visit the home to effect such a switch.

There also have been important developments in local programming for cable systems. Initially in response to federal regulations and subsequently to meet the demands of local licensing authorities, cable systems have steadily increased their facilities for local production. This programming is primarily of two types: Local Origination, controlled and supplied by the cable operator himself; and Access, programming produced by other persons and institutions in the community for cablecasting on channels set aside for such purposes, usually on a common carrier type arrangement.

The Access concept really began with the FCC's 1972 rules, and has ever since been an integral part of most franchise negotiations. The most visible type is Public Access, in which members of a community are provided a free channel, and often free production facilities as well, to programme on a first come first served basis. The programming must be non-commercial, and no censorship by the cable system operator is allowed. While provisions for Public Access channels are rather commonplace now, it is also common for franchises to call for other free channels for local government, educational institutions, or libraries and health centres. To date seldom encountered, but arguably by far the most important, is the notion of Leased Access channels, in which cablecast time must be made available at a set fee and a non-discriminatory basis to anyone for any purpose.

It is difficult to evaluate the US Public Access experiment, as it is unclear what are reasonable expectations and what are sufficient community cost benefits with such a service. How, for example, does one evaluate a programme produced by local teenagers to provide counsel for other teenagers with personal problems? Who knows how many young people are watching? On a given evening three people telephone in with personal questions, one with suicide on her mind, and she seems to be

helped. Is the programme worth it? Or would the
same amount of money be better spent hiring another
community social worker? Television programming,
even cable television programming, is not
inexpensive. A 'free' Public Access Channel is not
really free. The cost of the channel, and the
production equipment associated with it, are passed
along to the subscribers. Is this a reasonable
subsidisation?

It would seem that the free Access idea is
today entering an important test period in the US.
Cable companies are finding operating costs higher
and revenues lower than they had anticipated, and
as cost cutting measures are explored by the
industry, serious questions are going to be raised
about the necessity of Access services negotiated
during the heat of competition for city licences.

But while Public Access might be facing
challenge other forms of Access appear to be
developing. In particular educational and health
institutions are moving to utilize local cable
systems to reach the community with their services.
Also, local and state government are beginning to
realise the possibilities. On the federal level, a
public affairs channel called C-SPAN has been
operating for some time now. Although actually
under private control, the channel is largely
devoted to televising federal government proceedings
and public affairs programming. States like New
York and California are seriously considering the
prospects of a state level equivalent. In the near
future, then, it is highly possible that cable
television will be the basis for an expansion of
public telecommunications activity by government
agencies and professional institutions. Indicative
of what might develop are announcements by a major
labour movement and a major political party of
their respective intentions to develop national
cable programming services.

Local Origination, on the other hand, is now
becoming an important source of income for the
cable industry. With programmes ranging from local
news and sports to old movies, cable companies are
attracting an increasing share of local advertising,
even in communities with local television stations.
The programming is often of a variety that the
local broadcasting station feels it cannot afford.
The public affairs documentary with call-in
question period is not the kind of programme a
commercial broadcaster wants to have in prime time.
It is a perfect programme for a Local Origination

channel.

One development that has made local programming generally, and Local Origination specifically more viable for cable systems is regional interconnection. As previously noted, cable franchises are granted on a municipality by municipality basis, so a metropolitan area which includes a central city and incorporated suburbs can include several independent franchises and cable operators. Traditionally these cable systems have had little incentive to co-operate, but with the prospects of local advertising such systems are now banding together to provide a potential advertiser with a market wide reach. This interconnection has broadened the financial base for the production of local programming, and encouraged co-operative production.

This brings us finally to the matter of interactive or two-way television programming services. The development of the Warner QUBE system, along with a number of demonstration projects by other companies, heightened expectation about how soon full interactive telecommunications would be commonplace. The technology for such has proven to be both more complex and more expensive than anticipated, and the cable industry is now in the process of reconsidering how fast or even whether it wishes to fully develop the interactive dimension. Several companies have publicly announced the abandonment, for the immediate future at least, of former plans to launch such services. In other communities, the cable operators have chosen to employ technology being developed by telephone companies to realise two way capability, and this could indeed be the wave of the future. Whatever the route, it would appear that general availability of full interactive television is some way off, with neither the utility nor the financial support for such being clear at the present time.

As we move into the mid 1980s, then, cable television in the United States continues to grow and develop, but there are some serious challenges confronting the industry. On the one hand, there is the levelling out of new subscribers aquisition. Systems across the country are finding the 50-60 per cent penetration figure hard to breach. Further, with the rising costs of construction and the levelling off of income from subscribers, the industry is finding it more difficult to deliver on all the promises made during franchise competition. Cities and companies are going back to the Cable negotiating tables to more realistically define what is to be the shape of cable service in the nation's large cities.

In addition to such internal problems, the cable industry also continues to face competition from other broadband technologies, both old and new. The prospects of a national Broadcast Satellite service is becoming increasingly questionable, but DBS can provide service for fringe areas that are too sparsely populated to support cable construction at this time. Also, SMATV service to large housing complexes and MMDS service to other urban areas could undercut cable's market in the large cities where construction is so very expensive. A surge in VCR penetration raises other questions for traditional pay cable services. Such competition could retard cable expansion to the extent that the truly wired nation would then have to await the development of fibre optic technology by the telephone industry. The pattern could well be set within the next three to four years.

PUBLIC POLICY

The development of public policy for cable television in the United States has revolved around three factors: Local licensing, abundant channels, and monopoly. Some 35 years after the initial appearance of cable television systems in this country, many serious questions remain concerning the implications of these factors for law and regulation.

From the very beginning broadcasting was understood to be interstate in character, and the federal claim to jurisdiction was upheld by the courts quite early in the game. The courts reasoned that the technological characteristics of over-the-air broadcasting were such that even the weakest signal had the potential for crossing state lines. The federal government was also concerned with the interface of private utilisation of the broadcast spectrum with such public uses as military and transportation communications. The finite resource had to be centrally managed at least to some extent.

Cable television, on the other hand, is a closed circuit communications system that must use the streets and public ways of a given community. Private cable operators, therefore, had to seek the permission of local governments to use public streets to construct their systems. As the price

for granting such permission, cities were quick to
extend their police power beyond normal concerns
for structural safety to the character of the
communication services to be offered over these
systems. The right of local government to grant or
withhold such licence or franchise permission
continues to this day,although the FCC has made
periodic public claim that ultimately this
authority rests with them.

In 1966 when the FCC moved to restrict distant
signal importation into the nation's top 100
markets, a cable system in San Diego, California
challenged the FCC's authority to so rule. As part
of this rulemaking, the FCC had put forward two
jurisdiction claims; one based on their power over
'interstate communications by wire' and a second on
the notion that cable television was ancillary to
broadcasting.[14] In claiming ancillary jurisdiction,
the FCC pointed out that Congress had given the FCC
a mandate to see that all citizens of the United
States received as good as possible a broadcast
service. Cable television, claimed the FCC,
threatened the Commission's efforts towards this
end by potentially disrupting the financial base of
local stations through fractionalisation of
audiences. Therefore, in order to carry out the
mandate of Congress, cable retransmission of
broadcast signals, in particular distant signals,
had to be federally regulated.

The case brought by the San Diego operator
resulted in a victory for the FCC, but not a very
complete one.The Supreme Court ruled that the
ancillary claim was indeed legitimate, but then
failed to deal with the broader argument for
jurisdiction based on the supposed interstate
character of cable television.[15] The limited
character of this ruling became clear in 1977 when
the Supreme Court refused to review a lower court
decision stating that the FCC did not have the
authority to regulate Pay Cable, inasmuch as
broadcast signals were not involved.[16] Earlier the
Supreme Court had narrowly upheld the FCC's
jurisdiction over Local Origination programming,
with a comment by Chief Justice Berger that this
'strained the outer limits of ancillary jurisdiction
[17]'. By the end of the decade, in a case
challenging the FCC's authority to require and
regulate Access channels, the Supreme Court had
made up its mind that cablecasting was not the same
as broadcast signal carriage, and therefore could
not be brought under the jurisdictional umbrella

created by the Ancillary principle.[18] By 1979, then, seven years after their belated move towards full regulation of cable TV, the FCC was, for the time being at least, largely ruled out of the game except for matters affecting use of the broadcast spectrum.

However, the basis of the court's ruling in 1979 was narrow. Rather than fully confronting the constitutional issues involved, the court simply ruled that the 1934 Communications Act, as then composed, did not provide a basis for broader FCC jurisdiction over the new medium. Congress, for it's part, has made numerous attempts over recent years to amend the Communications Act to give the FCC explicit powers over cable television, but these legislative actions met with strong opposition from local and state governments. Some states had moved to create their own regulatory arrangements for cable (New York, Massachusetts, Minnesota, New Jersey, and Connecticut) and were not terribly interested in surrendering to the Federal government the power to govern development of these new communications technologies within their own domains.

In October of 1984, however, comprehensive federal legislation for cable television was finally passed. The 'Cable Communications Policy Act of 1984' amended the 1934 Communication Act, creating a new section, Title VI.[19] The passage of this bill came after much heated and protracted debate, particularly between the National League of Cities and the cable industry. While the final version seems to represent a genuine consensus, the Act understandably includes not a few rather general, if not ambiguous, statements which will be the focus of litigation for several years to come.

Much of what had emerged as standard practice in local regulation of cable television was left undisturbed. The major exception is subscriber rate regulation. By 1987 all rates are to be deregulated in communities that are deemed by the FCC to have 'effective competition' in telecommunication. Exactly how 'effective competition' comes to be defined will clearly be important. The right to grant franchises and to require Access channels and appropriate production equipment remains in the hands of local authorities.

Perhaps the most critical part of the bill, however, is a provision requiring cable operators to set aside channels for commercial leasing. Such a common carrier imposition cuts to the heart of the question of cable's status under the First Amendment of the US Constitution. Congress was clearly concerned with the potential monopoly characteristics of this new technology, and took the further step of charging the Federal Communications Commission with monitoring industry developments, to assure 'diversity of information services'.

In earlier rulemaking, the FCC tended to assume that cable television was an extension of television, and thereby subject to different restrictions than non-broadcast media. In fact, they have applied the Fairness Doctrine and the Political Broadcasting laws to Local Origination Channels, a move which many legal experts consider questionable, but which continues in effect for lack of legal challenge.[20]

The FCC's 1972 requirements which the Supreme Court overturned in the Midwest Video case were argued to be unconstitutional by the cable industry, but the court, as noted, did not render judgment on this matter. The essence of the constitutional argument is that cable television does not use airwaves, and because cable does not use a limited resource it is more akin to publishing. Further, the high capacity of the cable technology makes possible a far greater number of television channels in each community than broadcasting ever could.

In counter to the 'unlimited capacity' argument, others point out that the technology involved is basically monopolistic. While cable is not a legal monopoly, it tends to be a functional monopoly. Due to the capital intensivity of the technology, it is difficult for a newcomer to compete with an established operator no matter how poor the existing service. There are also construction obstacles that confront a new system which the first system in a community often does not have to deal with. Utility poles, for example, frequently do not have room for a second cable.

Thus, the debate will be whether cable television to be considered closer to the print media or to broadcasting for purposes of First Amendment law. If the former, then each operator would be allowed complete control over all channels on his system. If the latter, then obligations can be placed upon the operator to share his channels with other programmers. Public and Educational Access channels have become somewhat accepted by the cable industry as a public service price for the licence. Commercial Leased channels threaten the operators' business control, and are quite negatively regarded by the cable industry. Producers and programmers, from newspapers to movie makers to would be Pay Cable providers are, however, equally if not more adamant that they have access to this all important link with the audience. It is ironic that prior to the 1984 Cable Act only local broadcast stations have had legal guarantee of commercial access to cable, this through the still operative 'must carry' rules passed in 1972 by the FCC.

This monopoly characteristic of cable television points to the third area of policy debate: ownership. At the core of this debate is the technological fact that the emerging high capacity telecommunication system can handle much more electronic information than does the common cable system today. The same 'wire' can deliver television signals, videotex news, consumer catalogue information, telephone service, specialised electronic magazines, and so forth. In other words, formerly separate communications enterprises are converging around the same delivery technology. So the owners of such networks are potentially in a position of power far greater than the broadcast networks or the major newspaper chains. While it might be some time before such a situation actually exists, between now and then a number of industry ownership and control questions need to be worked out.

In the early days of cable TV, the Federal government was aware that the existing communications industries perceived a threat in this new technology, and might seek to retard or even destroy it. The telephone companies in fact pursued policies regarded by many observers as ploys to interfere with the development of the cable industry,[21] and broadcasters repeatedly sought restrictive legislation. Subsequent FCC rulemaking, now supported by Congressional action, limited the extent to which either the telephone industry or the broadcasting industry could own cable television systems. Telephone companies are prohibited from owning and operating cable systems in areas where they have telphone service. Broadcasters are not allowed to own and operate cable systems in markets where they had television stations, and the three commercial networks are prohibited from owning cable systems at all.

With the freeing of A.T.&.T. to enter into

competition for at least some new telecommunications services, however, a potential imbalance has been created, presenting policy makers with difficult short term versus long term policy choices.[22] For the short term, it seems appropriate to keep the broadcasting industry and the cable industry as competitors. Thus most of the ownership and financial control rules affecting broadcasting, networks, and cable television continue in effect.

However, this fragments resources that possibly should be allowed to combine to balance the economic power of the telephone industry. By keeping one set of players (broadcasters, networks, cable television and television programme producers) in competitive structure, do we run the risk of facilitating an easy pre-emption by the telephone industry of the whole field? Certainly this concern to balance the competitive mix is at least one reason for the de-regulation movement in Washington. Still persisting, however, are residual concerns about the power to the networks.

The complexities of this situation have suggested to some that the real legal battle with the new telecommunications technologies does not lie with the First Amendment, but rather in the realm of anti-trust law. Is cable, or its successor, a true monopoly? To what extent should it be regulated as a common carrier and/or a public utility? Is private control of such systems finally an acceptable idea? What about vertical integration; to what extent should the same company be allowed to control the entire process from programme production up through delivery to the viewer? The dilemma, again, is that the very technology which could extend the availability of television to new voices also has the potential of greatly reducing the centres of control.

Two further ownership questions should be touched upon in passing; public ownership and foreign ownership of cable television systems. At the present time there are a few small publicly owned and operated cable systems in the United States.[23] Although numerous large communities have given serious consideration to such an approach over the years (Syracuse NY, Cleveland Ohio, St. Paul Minnesota), no major city has yet followed through. In line with the US tradition of keeping government at arms length from the means of public communications, such plans have thus far proven to be unworkable for cities faced with the problems of

raising construction capital and guaranteeing
against political entanglement. It is possible,
however, that more governments will become
interested in taking over operation of local cable
systems if the private sector seems unwilling or
unable to fulfill franchise terms, or conflicts
arise in renewal negotiations. This prospect could
be further strengthened as concern for concentration
of control in the new technologies increases. It is
a question of whether private monopoly is
automatically to be preferred over public monopoly.
The other solution, of course, is to work toward
maintenance of some kind of market competition in
public communications, even though the economics of
the new technologies mitigate against such.

The matter of foreign ownership of cable
systems has been briefly considered by the US
Congress several times, but no restrictions have as
yet been established. The only serious foreign
presence to date is that of Canadian cable
companies, which have managed to obtain several
dozen franchises, including some of the large
cities (Portland, Minneapolis, San Antonio Texas).
The Canadian companies were successful in entering
the US market partly because of their more
extensive experience in local programming, something
US cities were very concerned about.

So successful have been the Canadian companies,
in particular Roger's Cablesystems, that the US
cable industry has - albeit somewhat hesitantly -
sought regulatory relief from this unexpected
competition. But if Congress has thus far felt
little obligation to respond to the Canadian
intrusion, the threat of another foreign entree
-Rupert Murdoch - stirred a considerable amount of
legislative activity in Washington. It would seem
the US government has been willing to let be as
long as foreign competition was a healthy stimulus
to the marketplace. When truly large scale foreign
control threatened, restrictive law was more
seriously considered. It is probably fair to say
that in the near future some general limits to
foreign ownership of US telecommunications facilities will be forthcoming from the US Congress.

Concentration of ownership in the cable
television industry cannot be said to be high at
the present time. No single company controls more
than ten per cent of the present subscriber
population. The top 10 companies only account for
45 per cent of all present subscribers. Nevertheless,
there is reason to believe that concentration of

ownership will increase in the very near future.
For one thing, companies can no longer grow on the
basis of acquiring new franchises. So to grow,
companies must take over existing franchises and
buy out smaller cable companies. A considerable
number of corporate mergers can be expected over
the next six years.

In the meantime we are witnessing another type
of ownership change in the United States, towards
market consolidation by companies. As previously
noted, large metropolitan markets in the United
States most commonly are comprised of a cluster of
politically independent municipalities - that is, a
central city and surrounding suburbs. As cable
television must be licenced by city government,
each of these municipalities or suburbs acts
independently when it comes time to choosing a
cable system. In some markets, the adjacent
communities have tried to co-ordinate their
efforts, while in a small number of states, the
state government itself has pre-empted local
authority and followed a regional licensing
policy.[24] The norm, however, has been multiple
cable systems serving a single market area.

This has created artificial division in these
markets, and decreased the economies of scale that
otherwise would be available to the companies
concerned. Now that the acquisition of new
franchise is no longer the primary target of
industry energies, movement is underway to
're-distribute' franchise so that individual
companies can concentrate their holdings in
selected markets. Of course while this does create
better economies of scale and integration of
communication services, it also increases the
monopolitistic powers of the companies, a matter
not lost on local governments and consumer advocacy
groups.

IMPACT

The automobile was invented to provide rapid
personal transportation, not as an instrument of
urban planning. And yet the automobile has had
profound effect on the way human communities are
built in Western society. The suburb and the
shopping centre are basically creatures of the
automobile. So it is with major technological
developments; their impact is often quite different
from that initially conceived by the creators.

A great deal has been written and said in the

United States concerning the potential societal impact of cable television. The clearest beginning point for this speculative projection was the publication in 1972 of Ralph Smith's The Wired Nation.[25] The years that followed produced a number of major reports from government,[26] industry,[27] and the private sector, and a continuing stream of articles and papers. All of this has, of course, contributed to a rather widespread debate and public awareness, and it can be said with considerable justification that discussion of public policy for cable television receives input from a broad variety of public groups and individuals, on both the national and local levels.

It can further be said that this public awareness has proven to be a bit of a burden for the cable industry. In many instances, public expectations have exceeded the performance capabilities of the industry. However, many of these same expectations were encouraged by the industry itself during the rush to obtain franchises. Companies would promise anything that appeared to influence the vote in their direction. Now that it is time to deliver, cable operators are too often finding that either the technology or the financial resources are not there to do the job. Whichever, the consequence has been a slowing of the cable evolution/revolution, and considerable disagreement on what safeguards are needed and how soon.

Another front on which progress has been slower than anticipated is public adoption. The results of audience studies would indicate that the subscribing public has been slow to accommodate their behaviour to the potential of the new medium.[28] As noted earlier, the first cable services were esentially more of what the public was already receiving from commercial broadcast television. While truly different programming services for specialised audiences have been slower to develop, it is also clear that viewers often fail to take advantage of the full range of programming that is available to them on their cable systems. The tendency is to stick with a small number of familiar channels (5-6) and not to use programme guides for systematic exploitation of the full schedule. Nevertheless, viewing diversity is occurring, as indicated in the diminishing network share of the audience.

The critical point about this viewing shift is that it signals the end of a programming philosophy that has dominated television in the United States for decades - programming for the Lowest Common Denominator (LCD). While there were only three networks, programming was designed for the widest possible appeal. Actually, the approach was more a negative one, namely to select programming that would offend or repulse the lowest number of people in key demographic groups. Television had proved itself an inexpensive and popular means of entertainment and relaxation. People wanted to watch _television_, so the real job of the network programming executives was to come up with programmes that would not detract from this ubiquitous inclination. However, in such a situation viewers are selecting programmes more on the basis of what is acceptable than according to primary interests.

The promise of the new multi-channel television technology was that now, for the first time, you could programme to people's first choice. Lowest Common Denominator programming only works in a context of highly limited choice. With greatly increased outlets, television programming philosophy has to change. Of course, this will not occur abruptly. The slowness of viewer behaviour change has already been noted. Indeed, it will likely be a number of years more before producers and viewers begin to fully comprehend and act upon the programming implications of the new technology. But the changes are beginning to appear.

Another industry sector which could be rather dramatically affected is television advertising. For one thing, much advertising on broadcast television is designed around the principle of low involvement learning.[29] It is assumed that, given the nature of the programmes involved and the public's use of television for relaxation, most viewers are not very attentive to the screen. (Indeed, the further assumption is that if they did stop to think much about what was before them, they might react negatively).

Such advertising again works best with LCD programming. It is not clear that it works well within a programming context where viewers more actively seek out programmes in which they are highly interested. So US advertising agencies might soon have to produce more commercials that are atttractive to viewers, and not simply unobjectionable. This matter is further complicated by the ability (and practice) of viewers to 'zip' commercials by using remote channel selectors to immediately change to another channel when a commercial appears.

Advertisers are, of course, also adapting to cable television on their own initiative. The increase in available time has encouraged the development of new commercial formats, such as longer 'informercials' in which the message is not simply about a product, but also about the problems or contingencies this product was created to solve. In similar vein candidates for political office are utilising cable to present longer messages to the voters. (For a variety of reasons, candidates have had a difficult time purchasing long periods of time on broadcast television).

Finally, advertisers are once more moving to become identified with specific programmes. When the 30 and 60 second spot commerical was inaugurated on commercial broadcast television, the pairing of programmes with individual advertisers pretty well ended. The networks had just experienced the terrible threat of advertiser boycott as part of the anti-communism hysteria that swept through the ranks of American mass entertainment during the 1950s. Diversified spot advertising would undercut the influence of any one advertiser on programming. Of course, the procedure simply substituted network censorship for advertisor censorship, and the networks had their own programming objectives, as discussed above. With cable television, then, sponsors can again go directly to the audience. So the market place, in this sense at least, is broadened by cable technology.

This particular change in the relationship of advertisers to television is an example of broader structural changes in the communications industry. There is great potential here for increased vertical integration. Time, Inc. owns and operates the third largest cable television company. It also owns the largest Pay Cable company. It is further a major publishing company. Another example is Warner-Amex, with operations in cable television programming, and motion picture production. Other cable companies are offering or developing their own security alarm systems, their own videotex services, selling computer hardware, and even offering specialised telephone service. The fear stimulated by such ventures, of course, is that the cable operators will eventually use their monopoly over the distribution systems as a means of controlling the market. The lessons from broadcast network hegemony in television programming are very much in mind. The efficiency of the co-axial cable (or fibre) as a means of distribution has all suppliers of information concerned that they not be trapped with 'old' technology when the wired nation does become a reality. So newpapers, broadcasters, producers, computer companies, telephone companies, and even oil companies are looking for ways to assure themselves of access to the new communications technology   One approach, and the one leading to vertical integration, is to buy into the technology.

The other approach, of course, is to seek establishment of legal access. With such, the structural constraints are by-passed, and the influence of the hardware owner becomes even less than has been true for broadcast networks and local stations. With cable's many channels it is more highly possible for a producer to find an outlet for his materials. Indeed, a producer might become his own distributor, even using leased cable channels to deliver programmes to the public. It should not be surprising to find that the broadcast and Pay Cable networks are moving more and more into production, possibly in preparation for the time when their position as monopoly distribution centre will no longer be a viable basis of business. The whole structure of the television industry, then, from producer through wholesaler to retailer, seems to be on the verge of undergoing some fundamental realignments.Few people doubt that the three commercial networks - NBC, CBS, and ABC - will continue to be a powerful presence in the US television industry, but it will be in a different market context than the one these companies enjoyed before the development of cable television.

This brings us finally to the question of implications for the broader society.It is interesting to note that urban planners were amongst the very first to recognise the implications of cable television and other emerging broadband telecommunications technologies.[30] At the centre of their interest was a projected transportation-communi-cations trade off.Many transactions that presently rely heavily upon transportation could perhaps more efficiently be conducted through greater use of communications. When a shopper commutes to a shopping centre, it is primarily for communication purposes. The shopper wants information about a product. The shopper provides information to the seller about the desired purchase. They both exchange information with the bank to pay for the product. Only the actual delivery of the product

requires transportation. What are the implications
for the physical structure of our society, the
urban planners asked, if indeed the shopper and the
seller communicated through electronic media rather
than physically face to face for this business
transaction?

Since these early ruminations considerable
discussion has been forthcoming over such services
as Teleconferencing, Electronic Funds Transfer,
Videotex shopping, and electronic mail. But the
question to be asked is not just of the possibility
of such services, but also of the broader
implications for institutional and community
structure. Will the work place be decentralised,
and how much? What job displacement will occur in
industries associated with transportation? Will the
'city centre' phenomenon disappear, and what of the
urban ghettos?

There is also concern that the new telecommunications technologies could have profound effect on
the social fabric of the United States if care is
not taken to develop appropriate policy counter-
measures. Perhaps the most often discussed problem
is that of a widening information and communication
gap.[31] The fear is that information is increasingly
becoming a market commodity in US society, and
public sources that used to be available on a free
basis to all-broadcasting, libraries, even education
- will at least in part be displaced by commercial
services in which the consumer must pay for
information received. Even sources of information
like newspapers which are presently available to
all at a modest cost, could become more costly if
their availability in videotex form presupposed
that the customer was 'hooked up' to the delivery
technology in the first place.

There is a political dimension to this problem
as well. It is speculated on the one hand that the
interactive telecommunications technology could be
used as a means of increasing public discussion of
public issues, along the lines possible in the
small communities of an earlier America. On the
other side of the coin, there is some opinion in US
political science that the complexity of modern
American society is such that true populist
democracy, as envision by the framers of the US
constitution, is no longer possible. Increased
communication flow will simply lead to more
'information overload.'[32]

Whatever the contribution of the new technology
to increased public interaction, clearly the

interaction will be among those who are 'on the cable'. While economic status can never be a determining factor in who has a vote in the United States, there are many other aspects of the political process which could be affected, such as access to information on issues, participation in opinion polling, and involvement with a political party. The entry of such groups as labour unions and political parties into cable programming takes on important meaning when viewed in this light.

There is also concern that increased use of these technologies could lead to a greater privatisation of United States society. With the prospect of decreased public travel comes the possibility of less incidental social interaction. This is not to say that people will necessarily socialise less in an overall sense, but patterns of social interaction could be quite different, as such would be much more purposefully chosen.

There is another side to this argument, however. National computer networks are being used by people in very social ways, providing interpersonal communication links that were not previously possible. So while it might be true that people will limit themselves to more selective contacts, that selection could be nationwide. Whether an individual's concern is for international civil rights or the well being of the natural environment, these new networks can facilitate communications with similarly minded people around the nation, even the world, as never before. The prospect will still remain, however, that persons who do not share mutually perceived commonalities will have a lower probability of interacting.

Another side of the privatisation concern involves the projected decrease in the prominence of the three commercial broadcast networks. There is a commonly held belief that the networks have provided a binding force in US society, through common entertainment and editorial experiences that we can discuss together and which serve as a meeting ground during important national events. The question is whether fragmentation of the viewing audience will take away this common experience which, be it ever so limited, is still important in a diverse industrial society like that of the United States. Black Americans will all watch the BET network, Spanish Americans the SIN network, and so on, with the national audience dividing itself up along, ethnic and educational lines. Other observers counter, however, that the so-called unifying experience of network television is at best a myth,[33] and at worst a very undesirable basis of national homogenisation.[34]

This brings us finally to the issue of privacy. The same technology that facilitates privatisation also provides the means by which the individual can lose privacy. Managerial and economic efficiency are gained through the use of computerised information gathering and processing systems. Pay-per-view service is perhaps the clearest example. A truly efficient and flexible PPV system would allow the individual viewer to select and pay for only those specific programmes he chose to watch. Normally such a set-up would be a bookkeepers' nightmare, but with computer controlled telecommunications systems it is quite easily managed. However, the information the computer gathers and stores on the individual for purposes of providing better service is also information that could be used by a third party to determine such things as the social values and political leanings of the individual, the consumer tastes of the person, or how the individual might be most effectively and efficiently communicated with.

The matter is serious enough for some to advocate severe limitations on the development and diffusion of these technologies. Others are hard at work to perfect technical and legal safeguards. Still others argue that neither legal nor technical remedies can guarantee protection against privacy invasion, and that society must learn to live with the risks along with the benefits.

It was noted earlier in this essay that there is hardly unanimity of opinion in the United States as to whether cable television should be viewed as a revolutionary development, or simply another example of that little French saying about things changing and staying the same. When the average cable subscriber in the United States today conducts a casual exploration of the channels coming into his home, he might not perceive anything dramatically different from what was available (albeit in lesser quantity) before cable television came to town. If, on the other hand, our subscriber goes through his programme guide carefully, and spends a little time with some of the more unique channels, he might begin to conclude that, yes, something different is happening here. As our subscriber takes note of the fact that this same co-axial wire also allows home

43

access to computer banks and provides him the means to participate in live international group exchange, then he will be gaining an even truer perspective on what this 'Cable' could mean to him some day.

The American scene might indeed appear chaotic, but it continues to feature a dynamic marketplace in which the short term efficiency of national planning has been somewhat sacrificed for the anticipated long term efficiency gained by allowing market forces freedom to operate.

NOTES

1. J.Martin (1978), The Wired Society, Prentice-Hall, Inc., Englewood Cliffs.
   Frederick (1982), The Communications Revolution, Sage Publications, Beverly Hills.
2. Don R.LeDuc (1973), Cable Television and the FCC, Temple University Press, Philadelphia.
3. FCC (May 2,1941), Report on Chain Broadcasting, Washington, D.C.
4. FCC (March 7, 1946), Public Service Responsibility of Broadcast Licensees, Washington, D.C.
5. FCC (1960, En Banc Programming Inquiry, 44 FCC 2303.
6. US, (1968), Committee on Commerce, US Senate, Subcommittee on Communications, Fairness Doctrine, US Government Printing Office, Washington.
7. FCC (1966), Second Report and Order, 2 FCC 2d 725.
8. Cabletelevision Advertising Bureau (1984), A Guide to Cable America, New York, p.15.
9. US (1968), Fortnightly Corporation v. United Artists Television, Inc., 392 US, 390.
10. FCC (1972), Cable Television Report and Order, 36 FCC 2nd 143.
11. US (1976), General Revision of the Copyright Law, Title 17, US Code.
12. M.Harris (1971), Television Consumption Behaviour: Channel Use In Relation to Channel Availability, Ph.D. Dissertation, Ohio University, Athens, Ohio.
13. Reader's Digest Research Department (August 23, 1983), N.Y. Broadcasting (December 19, 1983), p.39.
14. FCC (1965), Commission Memorandum on Its Jurisdiction and Authority, 4RR 2d 1707.
15. US (1968), United States v. Southwestern Cable Co., 392 US 157.

16. US (1977), Home Box Office v. FCC, 567 F
2d 9, cert. denied 434 US 829.
17. US (1972), United States et al. v. Midwest
Video Corp., 406 US 649 676.
18. US (1979), FCC v. Midwest Video Corp., 440
US 689.
19. US, Congressional Record, US Government
Printing Office, Washington, D.C., (October 11,
1984), pp. 14282-14297.
20. 47 U.S.C.A. 315 (1964).
21. G.H. Shapiro (1977), 'Federal Regulations
of Cable TV - History and Outlook', in The
Cable/Broadband Communications Book 1977-1978,
Communications Press, Inc., Washington.
22. E.Schmuckler (1984), 'The Ware of the
Wires', Channels, May/June 1984, p. 36. Also
J.Swerdlow, 'Why Is everyone Afraid of Ma Bell',
Channels, October/November 1981, p. 29.
23. A.M.Gibbons (January 1983), 'Cable's Role
Expanding', Public Power, p. 18f.
24. N.Y. State Senate, Cable Communications
and the States. Also S.A. Briley, 'State Involvement
in Cable T.V. and Other Communications Services',
in The Cable/Broadband Communications Book, Vol. 2,
1980-1981, M.L. Hollowell, ed., Communications
Press, Washington, D.C., pp. 46-48.
25. R.L.Smith (1972), The Wired Nation, Harper
Colophon Books, New York.
26. Cabinet Committee on Cable Communications
(1974), Cable - Report to the President, Government
Printing Office, Washington, D.C.
27. Committee for Economic Development (1975),
Broadcasting and Cable Television, New York.
28. V.Sparkes (1983), 'Public Perception of
and Reaction to Multi-Channel Cable Television
Service', Journal of Broadcasting, 27:2, pp.
163-175.
29. N.E.Krugman (1965), 'The Impact of
Television Advertising: Learning Without Involvement',
Public Opinion Quarterly, 29, 349-56.
30. S.Mandelbaum (1972), Community and Communications, W.W. Norton and Co., New York. Also,
J.Dakin (1972), Telecommunications in the
Urban and Regional Planning Process, University of
Toronto Press.
31. D.Cater (1981), 'The Survival of Human
Values', Journal of Communications, 31:1, p. 193.
32. O.E.Klapp (1982), 'Meaning Lag in the
Information Society', Journal of Communication,
32:2, pp 56-66.

    33. W.R.Neuman (1982), 'Television and American
Culture: The Mass Medium and Pluralist Audience'.
Public Opinion Quarterly, 46:471-487.
    34. G.Gerbner, L.Gross, M.Morgan, N.Signorielli
(1982), 'Charting the Mainstream: Television's
Contributions to Political Orientations'. Journal
of Communication , 32:2, pp. 100-127.

Chapter Two

CABLE TELEVISION AT THE CROSSROADS: AN ANALYSIS OF
THE CANADIAN CABLE SCENE

André Caron and James Taylor

Canada has now been cabled so long, and the
penetration of cable is so deep, that the industry
has had time for an infancy (bucolic, even), an
adolescence (complete with identity crisis), a
vigorous (if somewhat fettered) adulthood, and a
middle age crisis, where it seems to be now caught.
    Depending on who you talk to, the present
prospects of the industry appear to be either: a) a
nice long stretch of serene mature years before the
inevitable decline sets in or b) premature senility
and early retirement. These days you can make an
argument either way and find supporters.
    The issue concerns more than the cable
industry alone. To a significant extent, the
communications policy of the Canadian government,
particularly in the area of broadcasting, is tied
to the viability of the industry: it assumes that
in the medium term at least we shall have '(a),
i.e. cable prosperity and not '(b)', i.e.
stagnation. The larger issue facing Canada is the
extraordinary meshing of its communications economy
with the basic North American grid; cable
constitutes one of the most effective remaining
levers available to policy makers in Canada still
providing some measure of control over future
development of the system. It is one sector where
the exercise of some measure of sovereignty remains
at least feasible. Hence its importance.
    This paper will look at the historical
development of the cable industry in Canada, will
analyse some of the factors that have led it to its
present watershed and will speculate, mildly, about
where the industry is going next.

A SHORT HISTORY OF CABLE IN CANADA

Cable first appeared in Canada in 1952 in the guise of 'community antenna television' or CATV, as it was known. The first subscribers were residents of a middle sized, comfortable, middle class Ontario town, London, who were seeking clearer and more regular reception of nearby US television signals which were then the only ones available. That same year (1952), which marked the beginning of television broadcasting in Canada by the publicly owned CBC Radio Canada (Canadian Broadcasting Corporation), 'Rediffusion Inc.' also initiated a cable system in Montréal and offered subscribers access to two channels. The new cable industry developed fastest in the provinces of Ontario, Québec and British Columbia. Small communities near major cities such as Montréal and Toronto and others within convenient range of the US border were most likely to be attracted to cable services. Thus cable would become one of the few communication technologies not deliberately planned and developed through industry research and development.

Four main periods spanning from 1952 to the present (1984) could probably best describe the growth of cable in Canada. While the division into phases is inevitably somewhat arbitrary, it follows closely the model of the Woods Gordon report[1], although our fourth 'phase' initiates a period beginning when their report was submitted.

Phase 1 (1952-1961): The first ten years or so of the development of the cable industry could be described as a 'shoestring operation', a sort of latter-day cottage industry. Licensed by the Department of Transport, applications were authorised to receive a non-exclusive licence to operate a CATV system. The fee for the licence at the time was $25. The 1958 Broadcasting Act did not cede to the Board of Broadcast Governors (BBG) jurisdiction over these applicants. This was hardly a matter of great concern, however, since few thought the industry would really show any substantial growth, overcome its limitation to low penetration areas and expand into larger metropolitan markets.

Phase 2 (1961-1968): During the next six or seven years, however, the cable industry grew faster than expected; the popularity of US signals far surpassed predictions. Cable systems spread rapidly. By 1961 there were 260 systems and over 200,000 subscribers. A new phenomenon made its appearance, the urbanisation of cable. This was in vivid contrast to the US where cable was still largely limited to rural areas and was to remain so long after saturation had been reached in large Canadian cities. A number of factors, other than the disadvantages of unsightly, costly-to-maintain antennas, explain the popularity of urban cable: 1) the disruption in some major markets of off-air US signals by newly built skyscrapers and 2) technological improvements affecting cable service. An important policy question now emerged. Since the BBG required 'regular' off-air broadcasting operations to maintain a certain percentage of Canadian content there was now concern about equity: cable operators did not have to abide by the same regulations. Market fragmentation was also beginning to be an important issue in the broadcasting industry. However, although new cable applicants began to find it a little more difficult to obtain licences, few major changes were brought about immediately in the official regulations.
      It became evident during this period, that this technological innovation had stimulated a new era of provincial/federal jurisdictional dispute. The conflict came to a head when in the mid 1960s the provincial court of British Columbia (Public Utilities Commission vs Victoria Cablevision) declared cable to be under federal jurisdiction, the decision being based on the principle that it was impossible to separate the carrier from the broadcaster functions. Cable was designated a 'broadcast receiving undertaking'. Thus by the end of 1967, although the cable industry in Canada was regulated federally and although its legal definition made it an adjunct of the broadcasting system, it still did not fall within the provision of the Broadcasting Act. The jurisdictional issues were far from resolved. But while politicians stewed, cable was becoming more and more present in Canadian homes having reached about a quarter (23%) of them by the end of the period.

Phase 3 (1968-1983): Such a situation could only create frustration for the cable industry 'entrepreneurs' since, among other inconveniences, they experienced difficulty securing financial support. Other sources of irritation were the lack of exclusive rights and the judicial and regulatory limbo they found themselves in. Dissatisfaction with the BBG and the Broadcasting Act in general encouraged the Secretary of State to define a new broadcasting policy[2] and institute a new regulatory body named the Canadian Radio-Television Commission (CRTC) to replace the BBG.

The CRTC powers included attribution, modification, renewal and annulment of licences and policy-making with respect to special conditions such as transfer of ownership, etc.[3] A limit to its powers was set in that it's decision could be referred to the Governor in Council. Some CRTC decisions could thus be overruled by the Governor in Council, put aside or sent back for reconsideration. The Federal Court of Appeals would have jurisdiction with respect to decisions made by the CRTC.

Although there was a new regulatory body, it faced the same dilemma that had confronted industry policy-makers from the beginning. How does one define a system that is neither common carrier nor broadcaster but a hybrid with some of the characteristics of each? The broadcasting versus telecommunication dichotomy is not merely a conceptual conundrum; from it flows important practical implications.[4] Broadcasting depends on an exceedingly costly production system: as such it limits access to production facilities. Furthermore because of the high quality signal, receiving equipment is expensive. Telecommunication (telegraph, telephone) is cheap to access and receive, its investment is sunk into a technically complex and expensive distribution and switching plant.

Cable has broadcasting functions inasmuch as it originates community, educational and other speciality programming and is responsible for the content of the programmes it conveys. On the other hand, like a telecommunication service, it redistributes signals which it does not originate and is by no means technically limited to programmes or other matter having explicit cultural content. Revenues also come from subscribers (like telephone) and not from advertisers (unlike broadcasters).

Although essentially monopolistic in nature,

cable services are not considered to be a public
service by the CRTC; if they were this industry
would then be submitted to provincial jurisdiction.
(An exception to this rule is Bell Telephone
(CANADA) which is considered a 'national' public
service and regulated by the CRTC). Rates for basic
services are therefore set by taking into account
value of the service produced as against its cost.
The CRTC, however, requires cable operators to
provide a community channel[5] and regulates channels
devoted to special programming[6] although it does
not regulate rates for Pay-TV[7] nor for speciality
channels[8].

As this illustrates, it has remained difficult
to define the industry in terms of administrative
categories within the existing judicial classification
system. For many it turned out to be easier to
define what the industry _does_ than what _it is_. As
defined by Statistics Canada: [9]

> Cable television is a means of improving and
> increasing the reception of radio and
> television signals. It permits the reception
> of a greater number and variety of broadcasting
> stations beyond the receiving area of
> conventional radio and television sets.
> Subscribers pay a monthly payment and an
> installation charge which can vary according
> to the population density of the area served
> and the difficulty in obtaining and distributing
> the off-air signals.

Thus by the end of the 1960s cable television
had been officially included in the broadcasting
system; the endemic problems of the latter were
accordingly projected with new force onto the
growing cable industry, which having survived the
Scylla of unclear jurisdictional and definitional
boundaries found itself face to face with the
Charybdis of cultural nationalism. The first in a
series of hearings on cable were held by the CRTC
in April 1971. These hearings were in response to
concerns arising out of the threat of American
programming which was seen to be mesmerising
Canadian audiences and submerging native enterprise
under its cumulative weight. Interestingly enough
until this time cable had been perceived to be an
essentially English-language phenomena in Canada.
Not only did cable spread faster to the urban areas
of English Canada, it was also there that Canadian
audiences were most attracted away from Canadian

broadcasters and towards American stations. The
language barrier remained an important factor in
French Canada up until the mid 1970s; cable there
was more valued as a means to improve reception of
regular Canadian French-language stations in Québec
although increasing access to Canadian and American
television via off-air or cable was subsequently to
become an issue of the eighties even in French
speaking areas.[10] In Québec, for example, the
growth of the industry was much slower than
elsewhere and was more concentrated in rural than
in urban areas. This explains in part why a city
such as Montréal still has a lower penetration rate
(50%) than for example Toronto (77%) or Vancouver
(91%).[11] On the other hand, Québec, given the rural
character of it's early cable industry development,
continues to have a greater number of systems, than
other provinces.

Some very practical issues faced the CRTC.
Economic viability of the traditional broadcasters
was becoming an especially important issue in
smaller markets. It was estimated at the time that
12 to 15 million dollars of advertising revenues
was being siphoned off to American stations.[12] In
the meantime, total revenues for cable companies
had risen from 22.1 million dollars in 1967 to
228.6 million dollars in 1977, a 934 per cent
increase in 10 years.[13]

New policies for the cable industry were
introduced in July of 1971[14] and subsequently in
1975[15] and 1979.[16] Issues such as cross-ownership,
community programming, programme substitution,
priority ranking of signals, ownership of equipment,
compensation to broadcasters by cable operators
were translated into policies.

Some of the major decisions taken were the
following:

1. Ownership: Foreign ownership would be
limited to 20 per cent by decision of the
Government in Council.[17] Cross-ownership
between broadcasters and cable operators would
not be 'encouraged' unless one could prove
that it would not be contrary to the public's
interest.
2. Competition: Individual cable firms would
have exclusive franchises with well defined
geographical boundaries. A new quasi-monopolistic
policy was thus instituted.[18]
3. Licence amendment: Licences would be
granted for a maximum of five year periods and

amendments would have to be officially sanctioned for things such as subscriber charges, altering of entertainment or non-entertainment material etc.[19]

4. Service provision: It was decided to require, by regulation, operators to carry Canadian television signals following these priorities:[20]

i)   local CBC
ii)   local educational
iii) other local
iv)   regional CBC (unless it duplicated programme carried by local stations)
v)   all other regional stations
vi)   extra-regional CBC
vii) extra-regional educational
viii) community programming
ix)   any other extra-regional stations that do not duplicate higher priority stations.

In its policy and regulations the CRTC was reflecting not only concerns over cultural sovereignty and the viability of the broadcasting industry but also the prevailing social philosophy of the time. Thus the provision for community programming was especially important to the CRTC since it viewed a community channel as a conduit for involving direct citizen participation in programme planning and production. Providing access to the community channel became the responsibility of the cable television licensee who was viewed by the CRTC as playing the role of social animator in Canadian society.

Once the above priorities were met, American stations could be added. A 3 plus 1 rule permission was established: an import limit of three commercial signals and one non-commercial signal from the broadcasters in the US.[21]

In addition, cable operators were required by the CRTC to substitute American signals including advertising material by Canadian when programmes were simultaneously presented on American and Canadian channels.[22] The CRTC also encouraged the Federal government to change the corporate tax laws to reduce incentives to advertise on US stations carried on Canadian cable.

The late 1970s saw some experimentation with special programming channels. The policy aimed to assist Canadian programme producers by providing them with additional distribution opportunities. The return was at best modest.

While these policies were intended to encourage the development of special programming there was also concern to ensure that there would be no encroachment on television programme services being offered by Canadian broadcasters: each application was to be assessed by the CRTC on its merits. None of these policies, of course, resolved other festering issues which were to resurface during this period, most particularly the thorny question of federal/provincial jurisdiction. In the 1970s the provinces of Manitoba, Saskatchewan and Québec once again disputed federal jurisdiction over the cable industry. Québec for example instituted regulation by it's own 'Régie des services publics' in 1972 with very similar powers to those of the CRTC in granting licences to cable operators. The Québec arguments were of particular interest on this issue given that the province had exclusive and constitutionally recognised rights on educational and cultural matters. The dispute over definitions of the industry as either a common carrier or broadcaster resurfaced, since in Canada, in many provinces, broadcasting is regulated federally while telecommunications is regulated provincially. The issue was finally resolved when the Supreme Court in November 1977 failed to recognise any provincial legal or constitutional rights over the cable industry.[23]

If issues such as community programming and ownership were made central issues and dealt with successfully during this period, other factors such as pay-TV, MATV (Master Antenna Television), Canadian speciality programming and satellite services would only be raised, discussed and experimented with in the seventies. The CRTC on the whole adopted a conservative attitude to these kinds of innovations which remained to be resolved in the next major development period of the cable industry in the 1980s (1983 on).

Before examining the fourth phase, let us evaluate the consequences of the policies which were adopted in the 1970s for the cable industry. A number of positive points may be summarised.

The greater control over and better definition of areas of exploitation eliminated some of the uncertainties (over-wiring, duplication of service) that had affected the industry and thus reduced risk. This helped not only to change the industry's image but also facilitated financial backing and loans.

Although priority signal regulations at first brought complaints from subscribers, they did help to stabilise the Canadian Broadcasting System as a whole and may have further encouraged the proliferation of converters (augmenting channel services) in Canada. There were also negative factors. The slowness in granting new licences resulted in a certain instability since foreign investments had to be quickly liquidated. An even more serious consequence, from the industry's point of view, was that pay-TV[24] was delayed to the early 1980s; its real growth potential was in the mid 1970s before competing delivery systems became available (VCR, satellite). The waiting period of more than a year for fee increases has certainly also adversely affected the industry. Finally, the community channel cost remains a certain financial burden: it neither increases penetration nor directly attracts additional revenues.

Phase 4 (1983 on): Although Phase 4 can be arbitarily dated from 1983, an indication of an imminent period of redefinition in the cable industry and of new developments in the communication field as a whole could have been foreseen as early as June 1975. That is when the CRTC changed it's name to the Canadian Radio Television and Telecommunications Commission.[25] While it is hazardous to try to predict the future, certain key parameters of the cable industry have now been altered and have produced a new crisis. Where cable used to be the new technology, threatening security of broadcasters, other newer technologies have now emerged and present equally a threat both to conventional broadcasting and to cablecasting.

Policies on MATV's (Master Antenna Television) were promulgated in the late 1970s and stipulated that MATV systems were exempted, under certain conditions, from the requirement of holding a broadcasting licence. The cable television industry objected to this exemption and requested that an equitable regulatory treatment be accorded to all cable systems alike. In light of this criticism the Commission amended its exemption to permit, effective February 1, 1984, MATV systems to distribute all the programming services authorised for distribution by the cable television system serving the same area.[26]

In November 1981, CANCOM (Canadian Satellites Communication Inc.) first began to beam TV and other signals to remote areas, usually not served by cable. However, in March 1983 the extension of services to Northern and remote communities (via the satellite service, CANCOM) was amended so that US networks could be added to the existing Canadian signals available by satellites.[27] This can again be considered, as was the case for requests made in earlier years by cable operators, as a grudging response to the extraordinary demand for US signals.

Since January 1984, public hearings held by the CRTC have led to decisions on applications for licences to operate networks for the distribution of discretionary Canadian programming services. The Commission granted a number of Licences among these Muchmusic,[28] The Sports Network,[29] Latinovision,[30] and Chinavision.[31] Revisions to the year old pay-TV policies were also made, an acknowledgement in part of the failure of some licensees and a recognition of the limited potential of the Canadian and, even more, the English language market, so permitting the fusion of the two French pay-TV channels.[32]

Finally, the early and mid 1980s is a period where the Department of Communications (DOC) has become more active in defining it's policies and priorities. The interest by the Minister of Communications in creating a new privately owned French network and the bilateral agreements with several countries including France for co-productions is an example of this.

In retrospect, however, it is interesting to consider what options were not chosen by the CRTC in the last decades. Some of the more noticeable ones, identified by analysis of the industry,[33] are the following:

1. The decision not to opt for the 'wired nation' concept. With all the new technological services now being considered this is certainly a major decision that may favour other carriers for these services.
2. The non acceptance of cross-ownership between cable operators and pay-TV enterprises. This is an especially interesting decision in light of the fact that the same principle was not applied in terms of broadcasters and cable operators. Although there is an internal policy that also discourages the cross-ownership between broadcasters and cable operators it is allowed if one can demonstrate public interest.

3. Finally, the policy of not allowing advertising revenues in community and special programming service. As a result, since the penetration rate has reached its economic profitability level cable operators find themselves in the position of having to offer additional services to increase income.

From a larger perspective, the most significant 'event' of all was a non-event, the failure of pay-TV to take off. During the seventies, the CRTC held back on a decision to initiate more than strictly experimental pilot trials of pay-TV. Why it did so is not completely clear, but possibly at the root of the failure to move was a perception that pay-TV would be a bonanza. The CRTC foresaw the rules of the game being profoundly reshaped and national priorities being lost in the shuffle. When the decision was finally taken, the CRTC opted for a situation of controlled competition, leaving as much leverage to the regulatory agency to continue to influence programming priorities as possible.

The result seems to have surprised everyone, from overly optimistic industry promoters to overly apprehensive regulators. The market did not develop as quickly as expected, profit margins proved to be narrower than anticipated and the ideal of controlled competition began to appear increasingly unattainable. Why predictions were so wide of the mark is not totally clear, but there seem to be a cluster of factors: given the wealth of channels available on conventional cable systems, customers appear to see limited marginal utility in subscribing to pay services: other alternatives, in particular home video recorders and playback facilities, have made movies easily available. Satellite dishes bring sports events and a vast array of other television within easy reach of urban as well as rural viewers and while the net effect is not large it has impacted on markets such as bars and beer taverns. The nature of the film and television distribution system makes it economically almost impossible for pay-TV operators to supply the 'block-buster' for that draws viewers.

The instability of pay-TV networks (bankruptcies, mergers) has served to intensify pressures on the cable operators: if pay-TV had taken off in the mid 1970s, with something like the mass audience then predicted, it is possible the resulting benefits to the industry would have more than compensated for the profit squeeze that began to be felt as a

result of, on the one hand, market saturation
resulting in a fall-off of new customers and, on
the other, rising costs. Instead, as revenues
approached a ceiling, the industry began to change
under the constraint of the CRTC, as the latter
proved to be reluctant to grant rate increases that
would have passed on costs to customers.

In 1982, an even worse blow fell as the
federal government moved to combat inflation by
imposing it's so called 'six-and-five' programme (a
ceiling of six per cent increase in year one, five
per cent in year two), again practically freezing
cable revenues. As this article is written, the
industry is in some difficulty, hoping that new
services, such as speciality channels, will enhance
the revenue base.

OVERVIEW OF STATISTICAL INDICATORS

It is worth taking a much closer look at the
specifics of the cable industry in Canada in terms
of operating systems, subscriptions and revenues.

Operating systems. Over the last 20 years, the
number of systems in operation have more than
doubled in Canada. The most important increase
recorded, since accurate statistics are available,
was in 1978 when there was an 8 per cent increase
over the previous year.[34]

Table 2.1: Cable Television Operations in Canada

	1961	1967	1974	1978	1982
Systems in operation	260	314	375	463	564
Reporting units	N/A	N/A	329	408	475

Table 2.2 sets out the 1982 data in terms of the
number of systems by provinces.[35]

Table 2.2: Cable Television Operations by Provinces

	Maritime Provinces (N=4)	Québec	Onta- rio	B.C. (N.W.T+ Yukon)	Other Western Provinces (N=3)	TOTAL
Licenced Systems	63	185	143	94	151	636
Systems not Operating	10	6	11	9	36	72
Operating Systems	53	179	132	85	115	564
Reporting Units	48	150	117	73	87	475

Table 2.3 examines the distribution of operating systems by provinces and indicates that 70 per cent of all systems are to be found in the three provinces of Québec, Ontario and British Columbia.[6]

Table 2.3: Operating Systems by Provinces in 1982 (Total 564)

Province	Percentage of Total Systems
Ontario	23
Québec	32
Maritimes	9
British Columbia, North West Territories, Yukon	15
Other Western Provinces	20

The majority of cable operators are members of the Canadian Cable Television association, which represents 399 licensed cable undertakings serving approximately 96 per cent of all cable television subscribers. Some of the largest cable operators are Rogers Cablesystems in Ontario, 'Le Groupe Vidéotron' in Québec, and Premiere

Cablesystem (owned by Rogers) in British Columbia.

<u>Subscribers</u>. The number of subscribers in 1961 was above 200,000 and more than 500,000 in 1967. The number of subscribers has steadily increased over the years with the greatest increase in the percentage of households passed by cable being recorded in the early seventies (6 per cent increase in 1973 and 1974).

Increasingly saturated markets, however, for basic cable service is leading to a decline in the growth of new subscribers as Figure 2.1 clearly shows.[37]

Figure 2.1: Growth of Basic Cable Subscribers

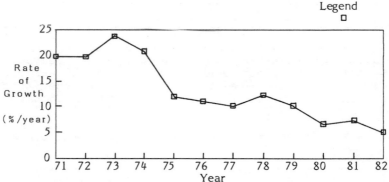

In 1982, 75 per cent of homes passed by cable subscribed to cable (58 per cent of total households). This in a country where 98.1 per cent of all households have at least one television set and where over 40 per cent have more than one. Of those with television sets, 87 per cent have one or more in colour. (See Table 2.4).[38]

Cable Television at the Crossroads

Table 2.4: Cable Television Market Penetration

	1972	1978	1982
Number of households	N = %	N = %	N = %
In licenced areas	3,711,649	5,866,366	6,895,445
	(59%)	(78%)	(83.5%)
Passed by cable	3,317,147	5,535,559	6,604,790
	(53%)	(74%)	(80%)
Number of subscribers	1,689,335	3,775,633	4,933,589
	(27%)	(50%)	(58%)
% of homes passed by cable who subscribed	51%	68%	75%

Looking more specifically at 1982 date in terms of number of subscribers by provinces one finds the following distribution (see Table 2.5).

Table 2.5: Cable Television Market Penetration by Provinces

	Maritimes	Québec	Ontario	B.C.+ Yukon+ N.W.T.	Other Western Provinces	TOTAL
Number of direct subscribers (i.e. no. of single dwelling billed directly by the cable operator)	263,655	964,444	1,629,624	679,981	706,525	4,224,229
Number of indirect subscribers (i.e. no. of subscribers billed under contract with a third party)	21,344	33,250	369,458	185,575	99,733	709,360
Total number of subscribers	284,999	997,694	1,999,082	865,556	806,258	4,933,589

Cable Television at the Crossroads

As one can see in Table 2.6, Ontario has the highest number of subscribers (41%) more than twice that of Québec (20%) which had the greatest number of operating systems.

Table 2.6: Number of Subscribers by Provinces

Province	Percentage of Total Subscribers
Ontario	41
Québec	20
Maritimes	6
British Columbia	
North West Territories	
Yukon	17
Other Western Provinces	16

To get a better idea of what services a cable operator can provide to its subscribers, Table 2.7 gives a profile of what is available to certain subscribers residing in the Montréal area and serviced by the Cablevision-Videotron group. Although the cable operator described here is among the larger ones in Canada, it is not necessarily representative of all cable operators. It is interesting however to see the full potential of services presently available to some Canadians. Fees and services (including various taxes) in September 1984 would be the following:

63

Table 2.7: A Cable Service in Montréal

Cable	
Installation fee:	$21.20
Basic Services (monthly fee):	$13.13
Extended Services with converter	
(optional) - (monthly fee):	$ 4.36

Pay-TV	
Subscription fee:	$23.11
Delivery fee (optional):	$11.56
Monthly cost per channel	
First Channel:	$18.44
Second Channel:	$13.81

Basic Service (Conventional and Specialised Channels

Radio Canada (French Public TV)	CBC (English Public)
TVA (French Private)	CTV (English Private)
Radio Quebéc (French Educational)	CBS (American Private)
Telidon information	TVFQ-99 (Television
Community programming	programmes from the
Weather/Time services	three state-owned net-
Community visual ads	works in France)
Tele-Guide (multi-screen	
presentation of programming)	

Extended Services (with Converter)

Radio-Canada (affiliate)	TVA (affiliate)
CTV (affiliate)	NBC (American Private)
ABC (American Private)	ABC (affiliate)
PBS (American Educational)	TV Ontario (Canadian
Tele-shopping	Educational)
TVEQ (educational institutions;	CVJQ (children, youth and
House of Commons debate	general programming)
(federal legislature)	Tele-information (news
TVSQ (sports and leisure	headlines and National
activities)	Assembly debates
Ethnic programming	(provincial legislature)
Premier Choix/TVEC (Pay-TV)	First Choice (Pay-TV)
Much Music (Pay-TV)	CNN news (American Pay-TV)

Revenues. If one looks at selected financial indicators over the last 15 years one notices that operating revenues and departmental expenses have steadily increased over the years, whereas net profit has sharply decreased in the last two years. Thus, net profit in 1982 has returned to the level one found in 1976 (i.e. approximately $18 million). The greatest increase in net profits after taxes was recorded in 1977 (25%) [39] as Table 2.8 shows.

Table 2.8: Selected Financial Indicators for the Canadian Cable Television Industry, 1967 - 1980

	Operating Revenues ($ milliions)	Departmental Expenses * ($ millions)	Net Profit After Taxes ($ millions)
1967	22.1	13.8	0.5
1968	31.3	18.6	1.8
1969	37.4	22.2	2.3
1970	56.3	27.4	5.1
1971	66.6	35.2	6.6
1972	82.5	42.5	9.2
1973	107.0	54.4	12.4
1974	133.4	66.5	14.4
1975	162.3	82.5	16.0
1976	199.2	108.2	18.5
1977	232.9	126.9	24.5
1978	273.2	152.7	27.9
1979	313.7	183.3	25.1
1980	352.2	202.4	27.3
1981	405.0	245.2	18.1
1982	472.3	288.5	18.2

* includes programme, technical, sales and promotion, and adminstrative and general expenses.

Other indicators of financial performances over the last four years show that operating revenues increased 17 per cent from 1981 to 1982. Operating expenses over the same period increased 18 per cent. Table 2.9 shows that direct subscribers accounted for 87 per cent of operating revenues in 1982.

Table 2.9: Operating Revenues - Total Revenue in 1982 was $472,343,767

Revenue from direct subscribers	87%
Revenue from indirect subscribers	7%
Revenue from installation etc.	6%

As Table 2.10 also shows, technical expenses account for the greatest part of departmental expenses.

Table 2.10: Departmental Operating Expenses - Total Expenses in 1982 were $288,513,978

Administrative and general expenses	38% of total
Technical expenses	44% of total
Programme expenses	13% of total
Sales and promotional	5% of total

Finally, one notices that departmental operating expenses account for the majority of expenses for every $100 of revenue which was collected (see Table 2.11).

Table 2.11: Total Revenue ($472,343,767) and its Distribution

---

Of every $100 of Revenue:

$61 go to departmental operating expenses
$17 go to interest charges
$15 go towards depreciation
$ 4 are provisions for income tax
$ 4 are profit

If one examines the cable industry in comparison to the broadcasting and telecommunications carrier

Cable Television at the Crossroads

industry, data as of 1980 reveals that assets are
overall quite small, that is, 3 to 5 per cent of
the total industry (see Table 2.12).[40]

Table 2.12: The Communications Industries' Assets in 1980
($ mln)

Telecom carriers	17,292	(89.3%)
Radio and television	1,398	(7.2%)
Cable television	674	(3.5%)

In terms of employment, the figures are also quite
similar for the cable television industry (see
Table 2.13).

Table 2.13: Employment in the Communications Industries in
1980

Telecom carriers	113,744 employees	(77.1%)
Radio and television	28,336 employees	(19.2%)
Cable television	5,396 employees	(3.7%)

Overall, the cable industry's share whether it be
in terms of assets, employment or revenue is quite
small albeit in the case of revenue it is, in
proportion to assets and employment, slightly
bigger (see Table 2.14).

Table 2.14: The Communications Industries' Revenue in 1980
($ mln)

Telecom carriers	6,254	(81.6%)
Radio and television	1,063	(13.9%)
Cable television	352	(4.5%)

DISCUSSION

What lessons are we to draw from this brief
historical account of the growth of the cable
industry in Canada?
        For one thing its triumphs and its perils
alike throw a very special light on the difficulties
of centralised planning and regulation in the
present technological environment. While these
difficulties are no doubt especially salient in
the Canadian context, there is no reason to think
Europe is exempt from the forces of technical
disruption of established conceptual and legal
frameworks. In Canada, as in Europe, the advent of
cable was greeted initially by public policy
makers with all the enthusiasm of 'un cheveu sur
la soupe'. As an industry, it offered no new
product. Indeed, as an extension of subscriber
antennas, the 'product' it did offer, insofar as
that term can be said to apply, is 'borrowed'
(some have used less polite language) from the
very people it has increasingly set itself up in
competition with. What kept the industry alive and
thriving, it could be argued, was the same thing
that made whisky peddling and rum running
profitable in North America during Prohibition:
customer demand. The image of cable has tended to
oscillate, as we have seen, between broadcasting
and common carrier; it could just as reasonably be
argued that cable is neither since it neither
develops original content (other than to conform
to the letter of CRTC regulations) nor carry
traffic of a general kind (and indeed in many
instances it rents lines from existing telecommunications carriers). Perhaps what it really is, is a
brokerage system. As a powerful broker, cable is
taken very seriously indeed by people with a
commercial bent; it is a source of chagrin for the
non-commercial sector, who perceive cable as
pandering to people's worst instincts (it must be
added that the larger American networks greeted
cable at the beginning without notable enthusiasm,
although they now seem to have come to an
accommodation). If cable has become respectable,
it is not because of a softening of broadcasters'
flinty hearts but because everyone now has to
admit that the presence of the cable brokers has
irrevocably altered the nature of the broadcasting
market system in ways that policy makers neither
foresaw or desired. This is a lesson which
European countries now entering the field would do

well to bear in mind

Most European countries have inherited a centralist tradition in communication, whether one considers either broadcasting or telecommunictions. While this approach is certainly familiar to Canadians and is reflected in the philosophy of some of it's main institutions, it stands strongly in contrast with the prevailing North American model. Centralisation is achieved by restriction, either because of the nature of the technology or through regulation, on the variety of choice available to users. Cable in Canada, has been a predominant element in the enlargement of customer choice. Because of its capacity, and hence its voracious appetite, it has exerted a constant pressure on the autonomy of Canadian broadcasting: the country simply is not capable of producing the content required to fill all the available channels and to meet the ever expanding customer demand. How this expansionist pressure affects traditional European assumptions about national control of the communication system is a fascinating area of speculation; it is at least doubtful whether policy makers in the European environment really understand the tiger they are grasping by the tail.

It may be that there is some general principle which says that what most people like watching on television is not what their regulators would prefer them to see. Cable as we presently know it offers the public a glossy, second-hand-like-new, unbelievably inexpensive product to customers who seem undisturbed about the manner in which the product was obtained or about the effects of their indiscriminate consumption on their own collective well being, economic or cultural.

In a way, the pattern of cable is not new. Communication systems have repeatedly developed faster than public policy makers could keep up with. Radio broadcasting set the pattern: the creation of the Aird Commission (precursor to the creation of the Canadian Broadcasting Corporation) was a response to the prevalence of American imports in the disorganised conditions of the 1920s. The CBC did not so much replace American broadcasting (which it imported extensively itself) as to redirect it. The creation of the National Film Board (NFB) came after the distribution of American films through American-controlled chains had become a fact of life. By the time Canada got into television production and broadcasting, cities like Toronto had begun to take on the appearance of

Sherwood Forest, so thick was the antenna foliage covering residential areas of the metropolitan area; the CBC entered an already established market dominated by imported American signals. A principal strength of the CBC, indeed, was its mandate to serve those areas where American signals were either not available (remote from the American border) or particularly attractive (in Québec where the linguistic barrier proved to be potent). Over the years, as cable has moved north to cities such as Edmonton and as the language fortress has been progressively infiltrated, even this second-level line of defense of the home-grown communications industry has been weakened.

With the possible exception of satellites, governments' recognition of the realities of technical change has tended to be tardy. The structuring of a broadcast policy around cable may have come too late to take full advantage of the opportunity of pay-TV, for example.

The key question is one of regulation. In general, when the word 'regulation' is employed, in the context of broadcasting policy, one tends to think of explicit regulations, such as laws. But the notion of regulation can be given a wider meaning. Anybody who builds a new channel, or a new thoroughfare, or lays down a new sidewalk, is in fact 'regulating' in the sense that the existence of a traffic-bearing system is as good a predictor of future user behaviour as any set of written regulations. In this sense, engineers and planners are just as much regulators as lawyers and accountants although they are not usually thought of in that way. If we accept this distinction, then we would have to say that Canada has had two systems of regulation. Furthermore, the effects of these two regulators have not by any means always been in accord. We have already noted that cable began under the jurisdiction of the telecommunications committee of the Department of Transport and under provincial public utilities boards more accustomed to handling telecommunications than broadcasting questions. Eventually, it is true, the CRTC became the depository at the federal level of responsibilities for both telecommunications and broadcasting and the creation of the federal Department of Communications in 1969, with its mixed communications, broadcasting and cultural responsibilities, created the conditions for a more coherent vision. The reality was, however, that the CRTC remained somewhat unidimensional in its thinking and DOC had difficulty integrating its diverse parts.

Cable has been an instrument of technological proliferation. For most people it stood for an enlargement of choice, an expansion of available cultural products, with few people much interested in the "Made in ......" label at the bottom. Yet the industry itself, although still notably profitable, is also fragile. It remains vulnerable to the same factors which assured for long its own predominance: substitution by a superior technology. Although there have been in recent years some attempts to produce technological enhancements, notably by Rogers and by the 'Cablevision-Videotron' group, who, for example, is developing Vidacom (an interface system allowing for interactivity between different technologies such as home computers, videodisc, VTR stereo and other services) these investments in prospective research have come relatively late. It is an industry whose investments in research and development have tended to lag behind its competitors. In the projected future market of information services, the channel capacity advantage of broadband cable systems is being eroded by two factors: the spread of fibre optics and the enhanced exploitation of existing copper pair systems.

Once again the stakes are high and it is a gamble for the cable industry which faces many dilemmas in updating it's infrastructure. If interactive operations seemed a natural choice not too long ago the reality of the costs of such an endeavour has now become more evident. Because of broadcasting saturation growth potential appears to be at least in part in data communication and institutional network services. But to do so it will have to either come into direct competition or enter into partnership with the telecommunication industry. It might, however, be more difficult to reach an understanding with these new partners than it was with the broadcasters of yesteryear.

Do other countries have anything to learn from the Canadian experience? Obviously it is not easy to generalise from one context to another, given the profound differences in history and geography. Perhaps the principal lesson to be retained from the Canadian experience is that the difference between an 'old' technology and a new technology is a matter of perspective.

We would like to thank Michael Tremblay and Lucie Audet of the CRTC and Mike Helm of the Federal Department of Communications for comments on an earlier draft of this paper. Also we would like to acknowledge Stanford's Institute for Communication Research and Harvard's Graduate School of Education for facilitating the writing of this paper by providing assistance to the senior author during his sabbatical year.

NOTES

1. Woods Gordon (June 1983), Economic impacts of this Cable Television Industry in Ontario, Ministry of Transportation and Communication, p.8.
2. Broadcasting Act, 1967-1968, Art, 1, chap.25.
3. Broadcasting Act, 1967-1968, Art. 16-17-18, Chap. 25.
4. J.Taylor, (1974), 'Le fédéralism et la câblodiffusion: l'expérience canadienne', Communications, No. 21, p. 170-183, p.174.
5. CRTC (1971), Canadian Broadcasting 'a single system': Policy statement on cable television, p.16.
6. CRTC (1975), Policies respecting broadcasting receiving undertakings (cable television), p.9.
7. CRTC, Decision 82-240, March 1982.
8. CRTC, Public Notice 84-81, April 1984.
9. Statistics Canada (1982), Cable Television, Annual cat., 56-205, p.7.
10. A.H.Caron et al. (1983), French-speaking Canadians and English-language television, Department of Communication, Ottawa, p.63.
11. BBM, Bureau of Measurement, Fall Report 1983 .
12. CRTC (1980), La radiodiffusion et les télécommunications canadiennes: l'expérience du passé, les choix pour l'avenir, Approvisionnement et Services Canada, p.43.
13. CRTC (1980), La radiodiffusion et les télécommunications canadiennes, p.41.
14. CRTC (1971), Canadian broadcasting 'a single system', note 5.
15. CRTC (1975), Policies respecting broadcasting receiving undertakings, note 6.
16. CRTC (1979), A review of certain cable television programming issues.
17. Broadcasting Act, 1967-1968, chap. 376.
18. CRTC (1971), note 12, p.34.

19. Broadcasting Act, 1967-1968, chap. B-11, Art. 17.
20. CRTC (1971), note 5, p.14.
21. CRTC (1975), note 6, p.9.
22. CRTC (1971), note 5, p.27.
23. Supreme Court Decision, Régie des Services publics vs François Dionne and the Attorney General of Canada, November 30th 1977.
24. CRTC, Decision, No. 82-240, 1982.
25. The Canadian Radio-television and Tele-communication Act, No. 2324, Elizabeth II, chap. 49, June 1975.
26. CRTC, Public Notice, No. 83-255, November 1983.
27. CRTC, Decision, No. 83-126, March 1983.
28. CRTC, Decision, No. 84-338, April 1984.
29. CRTC, Decision, No. 84-339, April 1984.
30. CRTC, Decision, No.84-444, May 1984.
31 CRTC, Decision, No.84-445, May 1984.
32. CRTC, Decision, No. 84-32, January 1984.
33. CRTC (1980), La radiodiffusion et les télécommunications canadiennes, note 12, p.49.
34. Woods Gordon (1983), Economic impacts of the Cable Television Industry in Ontario, and Statistics Canada (1982) Cable Television.
35. Statistics Canada (1982), Cable Television.
36. Statistics Canada (1982), Cable Television.
37. Canadian Cable Television Association Report (June 1983) Appendix III.
38. Statistics Canada (1982), Cable Television.
39. Statistics Canada (1982), Cable Television.
40. J.Braden and B.Shiell (1982), Cable Television Industry, Statistical Information Services, Department of Communications, Ottawa, p.27.

Chapter Three

CABLE TELEVISION IN THE LOW COUNTRIES

Kees Brants and Nick Jankowski

The mid 1980s will probably be remembered by
Belgian and Dutch media historians as a period of
conflict between proponents of the new media and
defenders of the old. This conflict centres, to a
degree, around the use of satellites and cables for
media distribution, and much of the conflict is
reflected in discussions of media policy.
    Many issues and themes find their way into
these policy discussions: regulation of the cable,
programming and services to be offered, financing
of the services, relation of cablecasting to the
national broadcasting system, and the influence of
commercial and international forces on the existing
media. In this chapter we intend to sketch these
issues in relation to the development of cable
television in Belgium and the Netherlands.
    We begin with a brief discussion of two terms
central to our perspective: control of and access
to the media. These terms are among the core
notions essential to understanding the development
of cable television. The second section of the
chapter provides a basic sketch of the broadcasting
systems in both countries. In the third section we
outline the primary characteristics of cable
television in the Benelux[1]: the rate of growth
during the past two decades, the systems installed,
the services provided, the regulations imposed. The
fourth section reviews experiments with local
origination of cable programming. Following this
review we consider three recent developments
related to cable television: satellite television,
pay-television, and the new information and two-way
communication services. The final section is
concerned with two themes central in the debate
around cable television - impact of the cable on
broadcasting, and access to the anticipated

abundance of information. Here we speculate briefly on the prospects for the cable during the coming five years in the Low Countries.

CONTROL AND ACCESS

Control has been a critical issue in the development of cable television and reference to it can be found in the earliest publications in the field. The Sloan Commission Report[2] devotes attention to ownership and control of cable systems; Tate[3] addresses community control and minority ownership of the medium; LeDuc[4] discusses FCC regulation of the cable in terms of media control. For the purpose of this chapter we intend to employ a general definition of control: the ability to influence decision-making regarding (policy issues around) cable television. Our intent is primarily to raise questions regarding control.

Access shares the same diversity of expression as control, and nearly the same importance among media scholars.[5] In this chapter we are using the term access in reference to the ability to participate in the programming distributed by a cable television station. These activities can relate to local origination programming; they can also relate to the new information and communication services. Access, as used here, is much more limited than control. Access has to do with making use of the communication possibilities of the medium; control has to do with determining policy for cable television. As with the term control, our purpose here is primarily to raise questions regarding access and cable television in the Netherlands and Belgium.

NATIONAL BROADCASTING SYSTEMS

For more than a decade the introduction of cable and its possible effects on broadcasting have been under discussion in Belgium and the Netherlands. Until recently television programming was a monopoly of the broadcasting companies, and the development of cable was dependent on the interests of public broadcasting. To understand this

development it may be helpful to outline the
broadcasting systems in the two countries: their
origins, their basic features, and the impact of
cable on the systems.

Dutch Broadcasting

The Netherlands has been renowned for its national[6]
broadcasting system which is to a degree open, but
also closed. The system is open in that - since
passage of the Broadcasting Act in 1969 -
organisations with enough members are allowed
broadcasting time. The system is relatively closed
in that six of the present eight television
companies which share the two television channels
form a core part of the so-called 'pillar'
structure which has characterised Dutch society
since the beginning of this century.[7] The main
ideological and religious divisions into which the
society is segmented are represented in this pillar
structure; little room is available for organisations
with other positions.

These pillar divisions have permeated into the
entire social framework: the political parties,
labour unions, the schools and universities, sport
and social clubs, and the mass media. Social and
political life took part within the societal pillar
to which one belonged. If a person were born Roman
Catholic, he or she would attend Catholic schools,
play or support the Catholic football club, read a
Catholic newpaper, vote for the Catholic political
party, and live in a house owned by a Catholic
housing estate. Within these pillars intense social
contact and control was exercised. Contact between
members of the different pillars was limited,
except for the elite groups of each pillar, which
engaged in over-arching political activity.

In the Catholic, Protestant and Socialist
pillars interlocking directorships were fairly
commonplace between the mass media and other pillar
institutions. The political party representing a
particular pillar played, of course, a central role
in such directorships. The media, as the primary
propaganda organs of the pillars, constituted core
elements in such politics of control. Representatives
in parliament, together with directors from the
media, were able to effectively determine media
policy and whether other groups could enter the
broadcasting system.

In this way, the political elites attempted to

maintain control over the information received and opinions formed by members of a particular pillar. This form of control was sometimes carried to extremes. An example of this is when in 1954 the Roman Catholic Bishops forbade members of the Church from listening to radio broadcasts from the Socialist broadcasting organisation VARA. Although the Church threatened excommunication to violators of this edict, it was difficult to enforce; few people seemed to take it seriously.

This pillarised social structure changed dramatically during the 1960s. A decline in church commitment coincided with emergence of the welfare state; rigidity in the political system lessened. Although similar changes occurred in broadcasting, television was, at the same time, one of the catalysers of these events. With the introduction of the Broadcasting Act in 1969 the path was cleared for other organisations to claim broadcasting time on television. The size of a broadcasting organisation's membership determined the amount of air time the organisation received. This regulation eventually changed the pillar alignment of the broadcasting companies.

Since 1969 two ideologically and religiously neutral broadcasting companies joined the other pillar organisations in sharing the television facilities. These two companies, with programmes directed at a mass audience and an emphasis on amusement programming, grew tremendously in popularity. This development forced the other more traditional broadcasting companies to re-examine their objectives and programming. Initially non-commercial and non-profit policies had been stressed by the companies, but almost all of them eventually undertook commercially oriented campaigns to attract new members: publication of glossy television programme guides, membership promotional gimmicks, and offering special leisure activities such as inexpensive group travel.

In 1984 eight major broadcasting companies shared time on two television channels. At the end of that year there were six so-called 'A' companies, each having more than 450,000 members. Four of these 'A' companies had their origins in the pillar structure just described. There were also two 'B' companies, with memberships between 300,000 and 450,000. Space is also allotted for 'C' companies, the third tier in the structure, having memberships between 150,000 and 300,000. No companies currently occupy this level. Commercial broadcasting companies, which rely on advertising and private income for their support, do not consitute a part of the system[8]

In addition to these eight companies there is the foundation NOS which co-ordinates the activities of the companies and provides technical services. The NOS also produces programmes which extend beyond the foci of the eight companies: newscasts, sport programmes and the televising of special national events. The NOS has no members; its board of directors is composed of representatives from the eight broadcasting companies, various cultural organisations and the national government. An independent chairman is appointed by the ministry which regulates broadcasting.

Broadcasting in the Netherlands is financed through licence fees collected from owners of radio and television sets, through membership fees to the eight companies, and through limited and controlled advertising. This last source of funding has been a major controversy in the country for the last two decades. Industry and business have generally been proponents of advertising on radio and television. A coalition of the press, broadcasting companies, and the Socialist and Christian political parties resisted its implementation,and - once implemented - its expansion. The matter came to a climax in 1965 when the government received a vote of 'no confidence' on the issue.

In the Broadcasting Act of 1969 a limited form of commercialisation was admitted to broadcasting. A special foundation (STER) was established for its exploitation. The STER was also authorised to distribute the proceeds to the eight broadcasting companies, and indirectly to the press as compensation for advertising revenue lost to broadcasting. Advertising is concentrated in time blocks before and after the news programmes for a total of 30 minutes daily, excepting Sunday when no advertising may be broadcast.

Belgian Broadcasting System

The broadcasting system in Belgium is organised around the prominent language divisions in the country. The system consists of the RTBF which serves the French speaking population in Wallonia. In addition, the BRT which serves the Flemish[9] speaking northern region - Flanders. There is also a small German speaking population in the country with its own company, the BRF.[10] The multi-party political system - formed along religious , ideological and social cleavages - also reflects these linguistic divisions. The three major political parties all have regional wings; only the Socialists attempt to construct a national political programme which transcends these divisions.

The programming is financed, as in the Netherlands, from licence fees collected from radio and television set owners. Distribution of the funding, however, is not equally allotted among the two main corporations: the French RTBF receives the full amount collected within its region; the Flemish language BRT must settle for 60 per cent of the fees collected.

Advertising has been under discussion since 1960, but its opponents have succeeded in prohibiting it until now. A form of non-commercial sponsorship of public services has been introduced, and the RTBF is experimenting with advertising without mentioning the brand names of the products.

The broadcasting situation in Belgium is very much determined by the cultural autonomy each language group enjoys. Since a number of reformist measures in 1980, both language communities have autonomous governments, independent of the national government. Although laws regarding cable television and advertising are still a matter of national governmental concern, two separate media policies exist side by side. The distribution of licence fees, as noted earlier, is an example of the way the Flemish try to control the BRT. However, where the Wallonian government seems to develop plans for the new media and the role of the RTBF therein, the Flemish government does not seem able, or does not want to develop its own media policy.

Other examples of this kind of initiative by the Wallonians and reluctance by the Flemish are found in local television experiments which are only being conducted in Wallonia, and the pay-television undertakings which are only being exploited by the French language broadcasting corporation RTBF. No decision has yet been reached as to what role the Flemish language corporation BRT may play in the development of pay-television, but in all likelihood it will be limited.

The BRT and RTBF officially exercise a monopoly over broadcasting in the country. In practice, however, there are hundreds of 'free' or 'pirate' radio stations in Belgium. In addition, so-called 'guest' programmes have developed,

designed to eliminate some of the monopolistic
control the two corporations have over the airways.
These guest programmes are made by organisations
representing sectors of society. The position of
the political parties in the guest programmes has
recently been strengthened. A government office
which is authorised to exert control over
programming is prohibited from interfering with
news broadcasts, and since 1979, with the guest
programmes.

The broadcasting monopoly and measures to
limit or remove it have been the focus of much
discussion in media circles.[11] Theoretically, both
broadcasting corporations are autonomous from the
state. In reality, however, they are under close
control of the state machinery. Political
appointments are made at all levels of the
organisation. A political balance is maintained on
the board of directors of each corporation which
reflects the relative strength of the political
parties in the country.

Since 1970 an effort has been made to
introduce within the BRT an organisation structure
modelled on the Dutch pillar arrangement. The
strong position of the Flemish council (in
particular, the Christian Democratic Party, the
CVP) and the amount of money spent on the
(political) guest programmes have been influential
in the discussions. In Wallonia, where the
Socialist party PSB is strongly represented,
emphasis is on strengthening the RTBF monopoly. The
effort to 'pillarise' the BRT did not materialise,
but it made clear the importance religious and
political party considerations play in Belgium.

CABLE TELEVISION: BACKGROUND INFORMATION

Cable television developed in the Netherlands and
Belgium for the same reasons as those cited for its
development elsewhere in the world - improvement of
reception and increase in the availability of
channels. Admittedly, the situation was somewhat
different from North America: reception was not
hampered by mountainous regions, nor were there
local channels available for import from one part
of the country to another via relay stations and
the cable. The terrain of both Belgium and the
Netherlands is - excepting the hilly Ardennes area
in the South East of Belgium - more or less flat.
In the cities, however, tall buildings produce
essentially the same reception problems as

mountains. And, although there are no local channels in the same sense as in the United States, programming from neighbouring foreign countries seemed attractive enough for importation.

In the Netherlands the standard package of foreign channels provided by cable companies includes two or three German stations, two Belgian stations, and a French or British channel. In mid 1984 cable subscribers in Rotterdam could receive nine foreign channels. By the end of that year the French channel TV5 and the British satellite channel Sky Channel were expected to be added to this basic package. The Belgian cable systems provide more or less the same number of channels - around six 'distant signals' - but generally more French than German channels. In addition, a handful of cable companies provide local origination programming. Since 1984 a few companies in the Netherlands have installed antennas in order to receive television signals from satellites.

The Dutch and Belgian cable systems have been almost exclusively used for one purpose: the relay of over the air broadcast signals such as those mentioned above. Seldom are different telecommunication networks in the Netherlands linked together or are other information services provided. In Belgium it is common that cable networks are connected, but the linking of different types of telecommunication networks is prohibited by law.

Although twisted wire cables have been used for radio signals distribution since the 1920s, distribution of radio and television signals via co-axial cables is a product of the last two decades. In the early 1960s the first master antenna systems were installed in Belgium and the Netherlands. Thereafter, the growth proceeded at a logarithmic rate. The rate of growth in the Netherlands was partially influenced by the large number of co-operative housing organisations in the country which installed master antennas and cable systems in the housing complexes. This tradition of co-operative or public housing also exists in the Scandinavian countries where cable systems have undergone a similar rapid growth. By 1965 less than ten per cent of the Dutch households were connected to a cable network; by 1970 that number had increased to 20 per cent. In 1980 about half of all households were on the cable, in 1983 this was 68 per cent, and the prognosis for 1985 is 85 per cent.

Belgium experienced a similar growth rate. By 1983 some 87 per cent of all Belgian households were connected to the cable. The expansion of cable systems is expected to reach the point of saturation by the late 1980s when between 90 and 95 per cent of the Belgians will receive television programmes via cable.

In discussing the growth of cable systems it is important to consider the various kinds of cables and types of systems which can be installed. Nearly all of the systems in Belgium and the Netherlands employ co-axial cable; twisted wires, like those found in England and parts of the United States, are no longer used. Glass fibre cables are being tested in a few experimental situations. It is not anticipated that these fibres will find extensive application in Dutch cable systems before 1990.[1][2]

Co-axial cables are installed in two types of sytems: the so-called 'tree and branch' and the mini-star systems. There is much debate as to which system offers the most advantages. In the Netherlands the tendency is to install the mini-star, sometimes in combination with the tree and branch configuration. In Belgium the tree and branch system is popular, although the mini-star offers more potential for interactive services and for operator control over signals sent to subscribers. A drawback to the mini-star, however, is the initial installation expense.

In the Netherlands, as of 1984, there were some 12,250 independent cable systems in operation. About 85 per cent of these were community antenna systems; the remainder master antenna systems.[13] Essentially the same situation held for Belgium in that year.

Most of the 12,250 Dutch cable systems are small, connecting only sections of communities.[14] There are a few notable exceptions. Amsterdam, the capital of the Netherlands, has a single antenna system for the city with - in 1984 - over 320,000 subscribers. This represents 92 per cent of the households and is claimed to be the largest single cable network in Europe. The cable system in Rotterdam served, in the same year, 205,000 subscribers.

Regulations of the cable systems falls within the jurisdiction of the respective post, telephone and telegraph (PTT) departments of each country. In Belgium licences are issued by the PTT to government or private institutions for exploitation

of the cable systems. In the Netherlands local
governments are allowed to decide what form of
ownership and control is enacted; the PTT in that
country formally grants permission to cable
companies to operate, and it controls the technical
quality of the equipment installed.

Subscriptions to cable television vary across
municipalities in the Netherlands. The monthly
fees[15] average around 12 Dutch guilders ($4) in
most metropolitan centres; in small communities and
cities, however, the fee is as much as 33 guilders
($11). Fees in Belgium are even lower, ranging from
no charge at all to about $5. Many of the Belgian
cable companies operate at a loss due to the low
tariffs, but these companies are often subsidised
by their parent concerns.

Royalties were, up until 1984, not paid in
the Netherlands. In that year the courts ruled that
cable transmission was the equivalent of 'new
publication' and royalty fees could be demanded.
It is anticipated that the fees will increase the
cable bill by about six US dollars per year. In
Belgium royalties have been paid for domestic
broadcasts; foreign programming came under the
copyright regulations in 1984.

Issues involving control dominate the discussions
in both Belgium and the Netherlands. The influence
of the national government is felt by cable
operators and municipal governments both in the
area of the hardware and software. The postal
authority (PTT) can to a large degree determine the
state of technology employed in the cable systems -
whether a minimum of 12 or 30 channels, or which
switching system is to be installed. The government
would welcome more control in this area in order to
encourage standardisation of equipment and reduce
unnecessary investment in diverse and imcompatible
systems.

The software of cable television systems in
the Netherlands is, in one sense, strongly
influenced by decisions made at the national level
within the Ministry of Culture (a division of this
ministry is concerned with media policy). This
ministry has the power - within the political
limits set by the ruling coalition - to determine
whether satellite signals can be distributed
through the cables, whether pay-television will be
tolerated, whether local origination programming
will be permitted. In another sense, however, the
Dutch government has absolved itself of further
concern with the software. Software developers,

thanks to the regulations enacted in mid-1984, essentially have the freedom to proceed as they wish.
   In Belgium, government control still predominates; there are two ministries of culture: one for the Flemish speaking region and another for the French speaking region of the country.

LOCAL ORIGINATION

Local origination of television programming was one of the first applications of the cable networks which went beyond mere relay of over the air signals. The term local origination of television programming refers to signals which originate at the head end of a cable network. Some writers[16] distinguish community channels, where the cable company or an appointed body exercises editorial control of the programming, from public access channels, where no editorial restrictions are imposed. In the Benelux, public access channels as such do not exist. Community channels, however, have been experimented with since the early 1970s.

Community Television in Holland
In the Netherlands the first local origination transmissions took place in 1971 in three cities.[17] The national government initially reacted with prohibitive regulation, but later when it became clear how much interest there was in this use of the cable, provision was made for a national, government funded experiment with community television.[18]
   This experiment took place in six municipalities and lasted some three years. Three research projects were conducted around the activities in these community stations and resulted in substantial documentation of the experiment.[19] The results of this work have been summarised concisely by various observers:[20]

- it was demonstrated that non-professionals could produce television programmes of interest to their communities;
- viewership of the programmes ranged between 20 and 30 per cent, figures comparable with those achieved by some national programmes;
- the programmes were viewed by a cross section of the population within the six communities;
- younger residents tended to become more

involved in programme production activities than older residents.

The results are mixed regarding the extent to which such programming contributed to the process of community development - one of the goals of the stations. The informational part of this process was generally achieved, but there is insufficient evidence to know whether, and to what degree, the stations contributed to the mobilisation of residents in community affairs - the second and more important aspect of the community development process.

The national funding for the experiment terminated in 1978. Thereafter, five of the original six experimental stations were able to secure alternative funding. There was much interest on the part of other municipalities and community groups to initiate their own stations, but the national government refused to grant permits for extensive experimentation.[21] The national government was, at this time, more interested in promoting experimentation with regional radio. Radio and television pirates - persons illegally transmitting signals - became active in this period. Along with the expanding interest in cable television and satellite communication, this pirate activity forced the government to react. In 1983, a White Paper [22] was issued which contained a new set of guidelines for, among other media, community television. The White Paper, along with subsequent parliamentary and ministerial amendments, set the following regulations for community channels:

.   the station organisation was to be culturally representative of the community in which it operated;
.   a national government commission was mandated to allot franchises for cablecasting local programming; the local government could advise the commission;
.   advertising was not to be allowed;
.   transmissions were to be made only through cable networks; low power ether transmission was (temporarily) prohibited;
.   financing of the stations was to originate from local or regional sources.

In 1982 local groups concerned with local origination programming formed an organisation designed to lobby for community television and provide support services to new initiatives.[23] Limited funding prompted most of the groups to consider radio in the initial stages of activity rather than television. Funding for the stations was perhaps the most pressing problem. Some stations hoped to receive support from their local governments, often in exchange for programming time. Advertising and sponsorship of programmes were, as noted above, prohibited by the government.[24]

In 1984 some 50 stations had developed formal organisational structures and bonds with their respective communities; 36 of these stations were transmitting television or radio programming on a regular basis. Another 100 groups were involved in developing such structures and bonds. By the end of 1984 a total of 50 stations were expected to be cablecasting local radio and television programming.

Community Channels in Belgium

In 1973, after several years of experience with video activity, local groups in Wallonia (the French speaking region of Belgium) attempted to use the cable for distribution of their programmes. Three years later the government agreed to permit experimentation with community television in this region of the country. Nine stations were eventually given experimental status. In the Flemish speaking region (Flanders) the government postponed approval until an integrated media policy had been formulated. This delay resulted in no experimentation with community television in this part of the country.

Several regulations were imposed on the Wallonian experiments. Programming was technically limited to social and cultural topics. The stations were required to reflect an ideological pluralism similar to that found in the national broadcasting companies. The programming was to originate within the community, was not to violate Belgian law, and was to be distinct from the national television programming.

The experiments were intended to serve three purposes: (1) to provide local information, (2) to serve as a social catalyst in the communities, and (3) to function as an educational service. No research has been conducted which systematically examines the achievement of these experiments. Comments from observers[25] suggest that the social catalyst purpose had only been partially realised in most of the experimental stations. One of the more difficult aspects of this purpose was the development of quality programmes made by community members for distribution via cable.

The third purpose, to provide an educational service to the community, has been a particular concern of one of the stations - Canal Emploi in Liege. In 1978 this station gained approval to distribute programmes via cable. The target audience of the station was the large number of unemployed in Liege. The city has the largest unemployment rate in the country. This aspect, combined with the high penetration of the cable - 90 per cent of the households - provided a broad base to experiment with educational programming.

Canal Emploi was concerned with more than traditional educational goals; the intention was to instil awareness in viewers of the social and political factors related to their jobless situation. The station was also concerned with stimulating activities among the unemployed and in promoting job training.

In addition to producing a weekly two-hour programme, much effort was spent organising small discussion groups around issues presented in the programmes. Various projects using this combination of a mass medium and discussion groups have been undertaken in the past years. One project involved language learning with the aid of audio-visual materials.

The annual budget for Canal Emploi was almost twice as much as for all of the other Belgian experiments: in 1981 this figure was around 27.5 million Belgian Francs, compared to 16.5 million Belgian Francs for the other eight experiments.[26]

Given the absence of empirical research, it is difficult to assess or compare the Belgian experiments. Boon[27] suggests that the experiments have been well-received in their respective communities. Attempts have been made to formally incorporate the community channels into the broadcasting regulations of the country, and to initiate similar experiments in the Flemish speaking region of the country. Neither of these efforts, however, has produced results. The experiments must be seen, then, as marginal aspects of the Belgian cable services.

RECENT DEVELOPMENTS

Local origination programming is but the beginning of what cable television has to offer. Although Belgium and the Netherlands lag behind some other

countries in the services provided, a number of
developments emerged during the 1980s which may
transform the importance and impact of cable
television in these two countries. Here we describe
three of these developments.

Satellite Television

One of the more prominent developments of this
decade is satellite television. These communication
instruments offer an enormous expansion of
available programming; they also pose a major
threat to the national broadcasting systems. Since
1978 the Orbital Test Satellite (OTS) has been in
operation. Formally a telecommunication satellite,
it has also been used, since 1981, to relay
programmes from the British television company Sky
Channel. The European Communication Satellite
(ECS), launched in 1984, contains twelve transponders
and also relays Sky Channel. The Dutch have
allocated their satellite channel space to the
private company Euro-TV; the Belgians have made
similar arrangements with the Swedish firm Esselte.

These point-to-point communication satellites
are an integrated part of an international PTT
network. The planned Direct Broadcast Satellites
(DBS) are also controlled by national authorities.
The Luxembourg government is involved in arrangements
with a private company, GDL-Coronet, to launch a
hybrid satellite which will transmit programming
directly to consumers owning a small inexpensive
dish antenna. The industrial group providing the
technology for this project involves major European
companies: Philips, Bosch, Plessey, and British
Electrical Traction. The satellite will provide a
multi-lingual network of 16 channels and is
expected to relay both pay-television and
advertiser-sponsored programmes. Once this satellite
is operational it is expected that it will carry
advertising and will thus conflict with European
government satellite policies which emphasise
non-commercial programming.

In Belgium the same restrictions apply to
satellite television as for cable television.
Advertising is banned: this means, for example,
that the British Sky Channel is not relayed on the
cable networks in the country. The non-commercial
programming available from the Russian satellite
Horizont, however, is being considered for
distribution by a number of cable companies. In
1984 only one licence had been issued for
distribution of satellite programming; the recipient

was the French channel TV5.

Restrictive regulations have been enacted for satellite television in the Netherlands, partially out of concern for the national broadcasting companies. One such regulation prohibits inserting subtitles or dubbing the programmes beamed from the satellite; another states that the advertising must not be explicitly directed at the Dutch market.[28] Sky Channel was active in the Netherlands before the regulations came into existence and, as such, has been in a favoured position. In 1984 some 13 cable companies were relaying Sky Channel programmes to a potential one million viewers. By the end of 1985 this satellite television channel anticipates a potential 4.5 million Dutch viewers. Whether this market actually develops depends on further changes in the governmental restrictions and whether other satellite and pay-television services emerge.

The NOS has played a major part in the initiatives of the European Broadcasting Union (EBU) to develop a common European satellite programme via the ECS. This satellite programme is planned for implementation in 1985 and will contain sports, film and news services. It is meant to be a response by the European broadcasting companies to the commercial satellite programmes. In the future the EBU programme will be relayed via a direct broadcasting satellite. The BRT and RTBF are rather hesitant at becoming involved - as are the British and German companies, but for different reasons - since the EBU programme will be financed through advertising.

Pay-Television

Pay-television, a well-known feature on cable television in the United States, is relatively new in Europe. In some countries like Belgium resistence to this use of the cable is considerable. In the French speaking part of Belgium there is discussion regarding exploitation of pay-television by the RTBF. The Wallonian government, under pressure of the Socialists, will try to strengthen the controlling position of the RTBF over the new media. In Flanders there are no plans currently, but the centre-right government of this region of the country seems likely to encourage development of pay-television by any organisation other than the Flemish broadcasting company BRT.

The Dutch government proposed pay-television in its 1983 White Paper.[29] Four years earlier the government had commissioned an investigation of the impact of the new media on the press and broadcasting. This study resulted in 17 specialised reports on aspects of new media technologies and policy issues. On the basis of these reports a document, designed to advise the government on media policy, was published.[30]

Much debate ensued as to whether and in what manner the government should react to the possibilities of the new media. The Conservative political party (VVD) and business interests were in favour of reducing government control and allowing private enterprise to develop these media. The Christian democratic party (CDA),the coalition partner of the VVD in the government, was concerned with maintaining its close ties to the religious broadcasting companies and with supporting the existing broadcasting system.

The government proposed in its White Paper[31] that commercial interests could develop pay-television. Public broadcasting would not be allowed to participate in this activity, but could - along with private enterprise - play a role in European communication satellite developments.

This proposal resulted in counter proposals, some of which were supported by a majority of parliament. One was that public broadcasting should participate in developing pay-television, and that a third television channel should be initiated alongside the two existing channels. The government rejected this and the other proposals, though it eventually accepted the possibility of a third channel providing this channel would not substantially increase the viewer's licence fee.

It is difficult to determine how pay-television will eventually develop. One restriction is that the programming must be financed entirely through subscriptions to the service; advertising is not allowed. Moreover, a portion of the programming is to be devoted to Dutch cultural issues: five per cent in the first year, increasing to 20 per cent within six years. The government has interpreted culture broadly to include the arts, sciences, humanities, and religion.

A number of companies have expressed interest in developing pay-television, but given the restriction on advertising they are hesitant to invest capital. In late 1984 eight companies were approved by the government to provide pay-television programming. One commenced with programming in December 1984; the others were planning to start in early 1985. Mergers or withdrawal of some of these companies is expected, however. Observers predict that one, possibly two, pay-television companies will be able to recruit sufficiently large numbers of subscribers to financially survive the initial period.

New Information and Communication Systems

Experiments were initiated in the early 1980s designed to assess consumer interest in new information and communication cable systems in the Netherlands. One of these experiments involves cities located in the South of the country in the province Limburg - a region wedged between Germany, Belgium and Luxembourg. This experiment is planned to extend over a ten-year period (1983 - 1993) and to involve some 90,000 cable subscribers. The national government is committed to investing around $25 million during the course of the experiment.

In late 1983, at the start of the experiment, more than 100 organisations and institutions had expressed interest in providing information and/or communication services via this system. Various educational, religious, social welfare, cultural and political organisations were among the applicants, as well as numerous commerical organisations. Most of the programming plans, however, were for one-way information services. A few conventional two-way services were also listed: alarm services, limited opinion polling, cabletext. More advanced forms of two-way communications such as tele-banking and shopping are not anticipated until the last phase of the 10-year project.

A special - and problematic - feature of this market-orientated experiment is that it is intended to be financially self-sufficient. The services, in other words, will have to be paid for by the consumers. It is this aspect - the funding of these services - which will determine the actual limitations of the enterprise. Unless the communication services provided by public institutions are subsidised by the government, few observers expect them to solicit many subscribers.[32]

Another nationally subsidised experiment is being conducted in Zaltbommel, a small town with 3000 cable subscribers. This experiment is similar to the one planned in Limburg: much of the hardware and software are the same. It is being monitored by a social science research project focusing on the communication changes which develop due to Cable implementation of the cable system.[33]

Various other experiments with interactive cable systems are being discussed in the Netherlands and, in all probability, during the second half of the decade will be actualised. Many will involve offering different programming packages - tiers - and some interactive services, such as alarm and polling services. One of the more concrete developments is an experiment with electronic publishing of newspaper stories, cablecasted to subscribers. Scheduled to begin in 1985, six newspapers will be involved in this experiment. For the first two years the service will be free of charge; thereafter subscription fees will be charged.

Another experiment in which the NOS in the Netherlands and the BRT/RTBF in Belgium are involved in is videotex. News, educational cultural and regional information programmes as well as subtitles for other television programmes are the kinds of services to be provided via the cable. One version of the service makes use of telephone lines and is commercially operated by the Dutch PTT. This service, Viditel, has a capacity of 120,000 'pages' of information. Interest in this system has been modest to date: it currently has some 10,000 subscribers.[34]

From this limited experience with new information and communication uses of the cable it is difficult to determine how issues of control and access will develop. In South Limburg an organisational structure has been created which provides for input from the local governments in the region, regarding both hardware and implementation of new services. Access has been encouraged from the local, regional and national institutions. But, again, financial uncertainties may limit the involvement of the non-profit institutions - schools, the Open University, cultural and social organisations - from participating in programme production. The possibility exists that the experiment will rest heavily on the contributions from private enterprise, and that this sector will in the end have access to and benefit from the communication system.

THEMES AND PROSPECTS

In the course of this chapter we have sketched the broadcasting systems in the Netherlands and Belgium, the development of cable television and local organisation programming in both countries, and recent developments affecting broadcasting and cable television. Various questions regarding control and access have been posed during this presentation. Here we want to dwell on two themes implicit throughout the chapter: the impact of the new media on the national broadcasting systems, and the anticipated abundance of information provided by cable television and the degree of access to it. In the last portion of this section we cautiously note a number of developments which can be anticipated during the second half of the 1980s.

Broadcasting: from Public Service to Private Interest

In both Belgium and the Netherlands broadcasting was originally conceived of as a public service, comparable to welfare institutions, the postal authority and the school system. Television was seen as having a general educational function for the society. Public control of the medium - in the case of Belgium in the form of a state monopoly - was considered necessary for fulfilling this function.

This situation allowed little room for commercial television. Antipathy to commercial television was considerable among certain religious groups and some political parties. For the socialists, advertising was seen as a capitalistic tool for manipulating the market. Christian Democrats in the Netherlands have prevented advertising from being shown on Sunday. They have, until recently, also kept advertising from being broadcast before and after the 7 p.m. news service on the grounds that such programming is inappropriate for children watching television at that hour.

In Belgium advertising is forbidden altogether. That is one reason why a proposed Flemish language programme from the commercial Luxembourg station RTL will not be relayed to cable subscribers in Flanders. But, surprisingly, the French language RTL programme is part of the standard cable package in both Wallonia and Flanders. The advertisements found on the Dutch, French and German channels are, strictly speaking, supposed to be blacked out prior to their relay through cable systems in Belgium. But, like so many regulations in this country, this restriction is not enforced.

In spite of these reservations, commercial use of television has been a continual topic of discussion in both countries. In 1969 the Netherlands took the first hesitant step in

93

combining two opposing entities: a non-profit foundation (STER) was established to regulate and administrate radio and television advertising - a profit making activity.

Currently the Conservative political parties in Belgium and the Netherlands are in favour of allowing more commercial interests and activities in the broadcasting systems. At the same time the resistance of the Christian Democrats and the Socialists to advertising is slackening. Three reasons account for this change. First, the pressures of cable and satellite television are substantial. Second, the media themselves can benefit by the commercial activities. And third, there is a fear that unless a positive climate is created, this potentially lucrative activity will be captured by foreign countries and concerns.

The consequences for the Dutch broadcasting system are uncertain. Some see these new developments as the terminal signs of an already antiquated system. Others[35] think it is possible for the national broadcasting system to thrive alongside various commercial broadcasting enterprises. Most indications suggest that the government will continue to encourage private enterprise initiatives in the development of the new media.

In Belgium there is also a growing feeling among the political parties that the public is not necessarily best served by state control. Consumer sovereignty, proponents of this argument contend, should be emphasised. The desires of the viewer should determine what form of programming is provided. In summary, a shift is evident of the role the government is to play in broadcasting. This will probably result in more commercially-orientated programmes.

Access to Abundance

A deeply rooted ideological tenet in Western countries is freedom of information.[36] Sometimes this is expressed in terms of freedom of speech and freedom of the press. This freedom - to disseminate and to receive information - is seen as a prerequisite for a democratically functioning state. It is with the help of information and the ability to share it with others that citizens are able to participate knowledgeably in the democratic process.

For a number of years concern has been expressed regarding the limited diversity of expression found in newspapers and television. This limitation was partially caused by monopoly-forming in the case of the press, and in that of television by the limited number of frequencies available for signals.

Cable television was seen as a solution to at least the scarcity of airwaves. With advanced networks capable of carrying dozens - sometimes hundreds - of channels, the sources of information could multiply and diversity of voices could be guaranteed. In a nutshell, the democratic process could be given a new lease on life with the advent of cable technology.

The 'Blue Sky' speculations of the 1970s became - in the Netherlands, at least - the emerging reality of the 1980s. More channels are available, pay-television is developing, experiments are being initiated with new information services - some of which are to be interactive. The question remains, however, to what extent we can speak in terms of an abundance of information. An equally important question is who has access to this abundance.

We do not doubt that the amount of distributed information will increase thanks to cable television: more programmes will be distributed, more channels will be added to the cable systems, and more intensive and efficient use of channel space will take place. We are not convinced, however, that this 'abundance' will mean more diversity in the available information.

The diversity of information - the programming - via cable television will tend to be limited because of two factors. First, production of television programming is already a multi-national enterprise - and there is no reason to expect this to change. The business is dominated by Anglo-American companies (French companies also have a share of the market in Belgium).

The Dutch government is not insensitive to this form of 'cultural imperialism,' or 'colonizing of the mind.' Pay-television companies in the Netherlands will be required to use a certain minimum of programmes of Dutch origin. Viewer surveys suggest that Dutch programmes are preferred above foreign entertainment programmes broadcast in the Netherlands[37]. Even so, this provision will not necessarily guarantee diversity in the abundance of programming. Dutch as well as Belgian entertainment programmes are produced with the same formulas as applied to well-known American productions. The language and setting of the productions may differ, but the plot, character type, and dramatic form are similar.

95

Second, both diversity and abundance will be
limited by the economics of the enterprise. The
costs of programmes and new information services
will have to be borne by the consumer. The more
limited the audience anticipated for a particular
cable service, the higher the market price will be
for that information service. We noted earlier what
a subscription to the basic cable costs in the
Netherlands and Belgium. An estimate of the total
monetary outlay for the software and some of the
additional hardware for this new media is provided
in Table 3.1.

Table 3.1: Estimate of Cable Television Expenses

Annual Expenses:		
Broadcasting licence fee	$	50.00
Subscriptions:		
basic cable		50.00
one pay-TV channel		130.00
two new services		130.00
Special Outlays:		
Adaptor for teletext		70.00
Antenna for satellite TV		200.00
total:	$	630.00

These figures are admittedly estimates. The
subscription rate to the pay-television channel may
vary; the consumer may consider no more than one
new information service. The estimates do not,
however, include the price of a video recorder and
accompanying tapes - a piece of peripheral
equipment deemed essential in order to benefit
fully from the advantages of an abundance of
programming. All in all, the estimate is conservative.
It is three to six times the current outlay for
television in the Netherlands and Belgium. Even
when other leisure expenditures are taken into
account - such as for the cinema, theatre, and live
entertainment -the figures remain high for Dutch
and Belgian standards. The question is whether many
people will be able, given the decline in consumer
spending power and increase in living costs, to
afford this abundance.

Certain consumers, of course, will be able and willing to pay for the new services. Businesses, institutions, and economically well-heeled individuals will be among the pioneers. But if the possibilities of cable are limited to these users, then freedom of information becomes a privilege of the rich and the contribution of the cable to the democratic process becomes a fable.[38] The extent to which the promises of cable television can be fulfilled - the extent to which cable can provide both an abundance and diversity of information - is largely, we would contend, an economic issue.

PROSPECTS

Prediction is always difficult, particularly when it involves the future, someone once said. Prediction regarding new communication technology is an especially precarious activity: recall the mistakes made anticipating the rate of growth of cable television during the past decade. Our purpose here is simply to recapitulate the core issues we have developed in this chapter which we think will be of importance during the coming five years.

First, there is no reason to expect a return to the level of control and regulation which dominated cable television in the 1970s. The year 1983 will probably be remembered as a watershed in Dutch media policy history: when the first hesitant steps were taken to contend with the forces - mainly commercial and foreign - pressing on the Dutch broadcasting system. Although there is no landmark in Belgium as explicit as in the Netherlands, the mid 1980s for that country will also be noted as a period when the national broadcasting monopoly gave way to various other media, including cable television.

Second, although change in the broadcasting structures.is inevitable, revolutionary change is not expected.There will be much at stake in the years to come: the place and value of the national broadcasting systems, the cultural autonomy of the two countries, the survival of the existing programme production industries within the countries, and the development of new Dutch and Belgian industries able to take economic advantage of the new media opportunities. Neither government - both centre-right political coalitions - will allow these stakes to be left completely to the unpredictable forces of a free market economy.

Restrictions will be imposed, and later lifted, and new ones will take their place. The media policies in both countries, in other words, are likely to remain in constant flux; the changes, when they occur, will be incremental in nature.

Third, pay-television will commence with a number of companies offering entertainment programming - somewhat similar to earlier developments in the United States. One - possibly two - pay-television services will survive the initial competition to claim a portion of the consumer's purse. It is unclear what effect pay-television will have on the programming policies of the national broadcasting companies. One possibility is that they concentrate more on producing their own Dutch and Belgium productions and spend less of their resources on importing foreign productions. Whether the national companies will suffer viewership losses due to pay-television depends on what strategy they choose in the coming years.

Fourth, community channels will increase in number in the Netherlands. In the larger cities the channels will take on an organisational form which provides a diversity of specialised local programming services: for public institutions, for minority groups, and - for the entire community - a local news service. Limited space on this channel will be allotted to citizen-produced programming, so called public access programming. Community channels will in general occupy a small portion of the total programming package available on the cable networks. As such, it will in all likelihood play a modest role in the viewing attention given it by citizens.

Finally, the proposed new information and communication services will be slow in coming, in large part because of the limited financial resources of most consumers. Experiments will be reserved for only a few enclaves in the Low Countries and limited in scope until a viable market has been assured. A dubious assumption underlying much of the activity with these new services is that people are able and willing to transform their television viewing habits. Currently the primary function of television is to provide passive entertainment. Many of the new information and communication services proposed, however, require an active involvement on the part of their users: viewers must search out information and, on occasion, interact with the cable services or with

other users. This level of involvement is foreign
to most contemporary television use. The question
is whether viewers will modify their behaviour to
create the 'home information terminal' spoken of by
some forecasters or whether the television set will
remain but an 'eye in the corner' dominated by
entertainment programming.

We are appreciative of the extensive comment
provided by Patrick Herroelen regarding the media
situation in Belgium. In addition, Geert-Jan Kemme,
Denis McQuail and Ruud van der Veen gave us
constructive criticism and suggestions regarding
the situation in the Netherlands. The final text,
with any errors of fact or interpretation is - of
course - our responsibility.

NOTES

1. For convenience we employ 'Low Countries'
and 'Benelux' when we are actually referring to
only two of the three partners in this unit. The
third, Luxembourg, is not discussed extensively.
2. Sloan Commission (1971), On the Cable
television of abundance, New York, McGraw Hill.
3. C.Tate (1971), Cable television in the
cities: community control, public accountability
and minority ownership, Washington D.C., Urban
Institute.
4. D.R.LeDuc (1973), Cable television and the
FCC.A. crisis in media control, Philadelphia,
Temple University Press.
5. F.J. Berrigan (1977), Access: some Western
models of community media, Paris, Unesco.
F.Jouet (1977), Community media and
development: problems of adaption, Working paper,
Paris, Unesco.
N.Jankowski (1982), 'Community television:
a tool for community action?' Communication, (1982)
Vol. 7, No. 1, pp. 33-58.
B.C.Schmidt Jr. (1975), Freedom of the
press versus public access, New York, Praeger
Special Studies.
6. Regional broadcasting, currently limited
to radio transmissions, also exists in the country,
but is not dealt with in this review.
7. A.Lijphart (1975), The politics of
accommodation: pluralism and democracy in the
Netherlands, Berkley: University of California
Press.
K.Brants and W.Kok (1978), 'The Netherlands:

an end to openess?'__Journal of Communication__ (Summer 1978) Vol. 28, No.2, pp. 90-96.

8. Commercialisation of the broadcasting companies developed in another manner, intended for increasing organisation membership.

9. Flemish is essentially the same as the Dutch language.

10. This company does not have its own television channel. Each of the other corporations - the BRT and RTBF - operates two channels, but the second channels are mainly used for broadcasting special events.

11. P.Herroelen (1982), __Een, twee ...te veel?__: kroniek van twintig jaar Belgische radio en televisie, Leuven, Acco.
D.Verhofstadt (1982), __Het einde van het BRT-monopolie__, Antwerpen, Kluwer.

12. A.P.Bolle (1982), __Het gebruik van glasve-zelkabel in lokale telecommunicatienetten__, The Hague, Staatsuitgeverij.
F.J.Schrijver (1983), __De invoering van kabeltelevisie in Nederland__, The Hague, Staatsuit-geverij.

13. As more and more independent cable systems are linked together the distinctions between community and master antenna systems in the Netherlands is becoming less relevant. See F.Klaver and A. van der Meer (1984) __Kabel en satelliet__, Department of Mass Communications, University of Amsterdam.

14. In the early 1970s plans were developed for a national cable network, but due to political and economic factors the idea was abandoned in 1975.

15. The spending power-and relative value-of the Dutch guilder is approximately equivalent to the dollar. The same ratio - three to one - also applies to the Belgian franc.

16. T.F.Baldwin and D.S.McVoy (1983), __Cable communication__, Englewood Cliffs, Prentice-Hall.

17. In Woenel, Melick-Herkenbosch and Amsterdam. For an overview of this period, see J.Tromp (1974), __Gekonkel om de kabel. Commerciele machtsvorming in een nieuwe medium__. Amsterdam, Wetenschappelelijke Uitgeverij.

18. We are using a number of terms more or less synonymously: community channels, community cablecasting, community stations, community television. For a discussion of these and other terms see N.Jankowski (1982b), __Communication__, (1982).

Cable Television in the Low Countries

19. T.Koole, J.Oorburg and W.Wartena (1976), Lokale televisie in Deventer, en experiment-begeleidend onderzoek, Groningen, Sociology Institute, State University.
    N.Jankowski (1982a), Lokale omroep Bijlmer-meer. Eindverslag van een veldonderzoek, Amsterdam, SISWO.
    J.Stappers, E.Hollander and H.Manders (1977), Vier experimenten met lokale omroep, tweede interimrapportage, Institute of Mass Communications, University of Nijmegen.

20. D.Gorter, N.Jankowski and T.Maesser (1978), 'Lokale kabelomroep, de experimenten in Nederland en hun mogelijk vervolg', Intermediair, (September 1978), pp. 43-53.
    H.J.Manders and P.de Wit (1983), 'Lokale omroepaktiviteiten in Nederland', Massacommunicatie, (June 1983) 11, 3, pp. 159-168.

21. Permits were granted for cablecasting special events of short duration, such as local debates, elections or commemorative occasions.

22. WVC (Ministerie van Welzijn, Volksgezondheid en Cultuur) (1983), Medianota, 18 035, No. 1, The Hague.

23. This organisation, Local Broadcasters in the Netherlands (OLON), has its counterparts in England (ComCom and Relay magazine) and in the US (National Federation of Local Cable Programmers), but there is no similar organisation in Belgium.

24. Many observers anticipate that this restriction will eventually be lifted.

25. J.Boon (1982), Experimenten met lokale televisie en gemeenschapstelevisie in Franstalig Belgie, Thesis, Leuven, Catholic University, Belgium.

26. A portion of the funding for Canal Emploi came from the EEC, creating the situation in which an international agency provided funding for a community television project.

27. J.Boon (1982), Experimenten met lokale televisie.

28. It is disputable whether such regulations are legal; some observers anticipate further modification, or even elimination, of the regulations.

29. WVC (1983), Medianota.

30. WRR (Wetenschappelijke Raad voor het Regeringsbeleid) (1982), Samenhangend mediabeleid, The Hague.

31. WVC (1983), Medianota.

32. A review by Becker of interactive cable

television services in the US suggests a sombre outcome for this Dutch experiment. He concludes that experiments dictated by market forces produce programming - interactive or otherwise - primarily beneficial to the involved commercial interests, not the community. See, Becker, L.B. (1984), 'Social implications of interactive cable: a decade of research'. Paper presented at the forum 'Advanced wired cities: driving forces and social implications', Annenburg School of Communications, Washington, July 1984.

33. J.Stappers, E.Hollander and N.Jankowski (1984), 'Researching cable television in Zaltbommel; a community study in changing communication pattern'. Conference paper, International Association for Mass Communication Research, Prague (September 1984).

34. Considerable growth, however, is expected with a recently marketed interface between home microcomputers and this system.

35. H.De Bock (1984), 'Kijken naar (kabel) kijkers' Presentation at national cable television congress, The Hague, Hilversum, Nederlandse Omroep Stichting, May 1984.

36. There is much literature related to this theme. See S. MacBride (1980), Many voices, one world, Paris, Unesco; and I.de Sola Pool (1983), Technologies of freedom, Cambridge, Mass.

37. H.De Bock (1984), 'Kijken naar (kabel) kijkers'.

38. B.Heiller and K.Kalba (eds) (Winter 1972), 'The Cable fable', Yale Review of Law and Social Action, Vol. 2, No.2.

Chapter Four

CABLE TELEVISION IN GREAT BRITAIN

Ralph Negrine

INTRODUCTION

> The (wireless exchanges) system contains
> within it forces which, if uncontrolled will
> be disruptive of the spirit and intention of
> the BBC's Charter. The persons in charge of
> Wireless Exchanges have power to alter
> entirely the general spirit of the BBC's
> programme policy...The BBC has always regarded
> entertainment as an important part of its
> work, but has declined to devote its
> programmes entirely to amusement. This policy
> has been upheld by public opinion, and has
> already resulted in an acknowledged improvement
> in public taste.[1]

The history of cable television in Britain is
rarely discussed within the context of the
historical development of British broadcasting.[2] As
a result, its appearance (or perhaps reappearance)
is that of a new development and even a motor of
the information technology age. Though its present
guise is obviously determined by the state of
technological advance, the essential principles -
the social arrangements if not the technological
make-up - of relay services of the 1920s and 1930s
are not very different from today's cable systems.
Indeed, some current systems of delivery trace
their history to this earlier period.
An historical account of this technology
offers not only an intrinsically interesting
example of the social and political implications of
new developments, but it also illustrates the
nature of the medium in the context of the
development of British broadcasting. Relay systems
were designed to deliver clear radio signals to

103

those in outlying districts who found it difficult to receive broadcast signals through ordinary means. An additional attraction was their capacity to deliver foreign, that is, non-BBC services. Even in the 1920s and early 1930s their gradual expansion was deemed to pose a serious threat to the established BBC (as the above quote demonstrates). In his account of this period Briggs refers to the relay (later, cable) industry as the 'third force' in broadcasting. It was placed between the BBC on the one hand and the commercial (largely foreign) broadcasting interests on the other. For Briggs, the resolution of the conflict between monopoly and alternative (foreign and commercial) broadcasting was part of the 'haute politique' in the development of broadcasting in Britain.[3]

Today, as Britain embarks on the development of cable systems many of the issues and concerns raised in an earlier epoch are again being heard. One central concern today (as it was in the past) is the debate about contrasting principles in broadcasting. Briefly, it is a debate about on the one hand a regulated system of broadcasting imbued with a sense of social responsibility and, on the other, an unregulated and commercial system. The aim of this chapter is to explore these different systems and, subsequently, to trace the re-emergence of cable television in the 1980s. Finally, this chapter will examine the current development of cable television in Britain and its likely impact on British broadcasting.

THE EARLY YEARS OF BROADCASTING: THE BBC AND RADIO RELAY

The notion of 'Public Service Broadcasting', as enshrined in BBC mythology, is comprised of a particular approach to the task of broadcasting. At the heart of this approach is a view of the BBC as the 'main instrument of national broadcasting' with a commensurate duty of elevating public taste. Its 'education, entertainment and information' philosophy is one that places it at the forefront of cultural change.

Importantly, the BBC was able to adopt this stance because of its monopolistic position in British broadcasting and its insulation from the forces of the market. Its dependence on a guaranteed licence fee payable by all possessors of radio (and later, television) receivers put it in the enviable position of being able to undertake and encourage a whole range of programmes, 'the best of everything', irrespective of their mass or popular appeal.

From this position of strength - institutionally and indeed politically - the BBC determined and directed British broadcasting, first in radio and then in television. Its monopoly was finally broken in 1954 when the Independent Television services were introduced. But despite the break in the monopoly British broadcasting remained a heavily regulated system: only two authorities, the BBC and ITA (later, IBA), both set up by Parliament, were delegated with the task of running the broadcasting services and they, in turn, ensured that certain obligations were met. Radio and television services were designated as 'public services for the dissemination of information, education and entertainment' and programmes had to 'maintain a high standard...as regard their quality and content, and a proper balance and wide range of subject matter...'.[4] Such well balanced services were also, in principle, to be made available to the whole population. No part of the British Isles was to remain outside the blanket of coverage and so an element of equity was introduced into the system by ensuring that everyone had access to public and commercial services.

In the early years of radio broadcasting, however, the BBC's position was almost impregnable. The attempts by the radio relay industry - roughly in the period 1925 to 1940 - to break this monopoly and effective control over what the public could listen to had failed largely because the public service broadcasting philosophy had become so entrenched and powerful.

Some of the early clashes between the BBC and the relay operators illustrate both the BBC's position and its anathema to the contrasting position of the relay operators: a position based on the belief that listeners should dictate their choice of programme material. The BBC's response to attempts to liberalise the controls on, and regulation of, radio relays neatly summarises the core of the dispute with the Post Office (the licensing body for all broadcasting services) and relay operators and its continuing efforts to dictate programme policy in Britain. In a letter to the Post Office in 1932, the BBC Chairman wrote:

> The Corporation is surprised that it should be considered either possible or desirable for the choice (of programmes) to be regulated in

detail by the subscribers. This is entirely at
variance with the Corporation's policy and
experience and with the desire in the Charter
which enjoins that the service should be
developed to the best advantage in the
national interest .[5]

BBC pressure forced the Post Office to issue
restrictive licences to the relay operators. The
1939 regulations, for example, forced operators of
two channel services to carry 1 BBC programme and
75 per cent BBC output on the other service; one
programme systems had to distribute BBC programmes
for 90 per cent of the time. Despite these and
other restrictions, radio relay continued to expand
and, as with the early relay television systems,
the attraction of radio relay was not too difficult
to uncover. This was, primarily, the ability to
receive clear signals where none were available.
One can still discern from this historical
example what has remained of central concern since
then and that is the potential damage that relay
services could inflict on a structure of broadcasting
founded on principles of 'public service'. Relay,
from the beginning, was a medium for the diffusion
of signals; signals originated elsewhere. There was
never any attempt by relay operators to originate
programmes. Their profitability stemmed from their
ability to diffuse other organisation's signals
without incurring any of the expense of programme
production. In this sense, the medium has always
been exploitative and entrepreneurial: an enterprise
of 'middlemen'.[6]
Under such circumstances, it was not surprising
that the regulatory framework should have enforced
rather than weakened the structure of broadcasting.
Allowing relay services a free reign would have
opened the door to drastic change. Those with no
obligations towards public services or the quality
of programmes would, it was argued, only diffuse
that which was commercially popular. The logic of
this argument, and particularly the implied
antithesis between public service broadcasting and
commercialism has, in fact, been central to British
broadcasting policy making. After the 2nd World
War, change did eventually come to British
broadcasting. Commercial television was followed by
expansion in local BBC and commercial radio but for
relay the changes were much less visible though
just as important. From the date of construction of
the first television relay system in 1951 onwards,

there was a gradual shift to televison relay within the industry as a whole. Sound relay began to decline in importance as television and sound systems developed: by the end of 1971, there were about 1.8 million subscribers (or about 11 per cent of total broadcast licences).

But the television relay operators were working under conditions which were strikingly similar to those which faced the radio relay operators. The terms of their operating licences forced them to carry (or more properly relay) only those BBC and ITV broadcast signals available locally. They were not even allowed to 'import' signals from non-adjacent commercial television regions. Their role was simply that of a supplementary technology which was useful in extending the coverage of the broadcasting authorities in bad reception areas.

This period of growth of television relay was marked by a number of attempts to shed the plethora of restrictions imposed by the Post Office. However, neither those who advised successive governments, nor those with a vested interest in the existing system of broadcasting, saw the need for a less restrictive policy. Indeed, none of the broadcasting inquiries after 1945 - that of 1951[7], 1960[8] or 1977[9] - recommended a liberalisation of policies towards cable.

Even the 1977 inquiry into 'the future of broadcasting' was rather dismissive of cable television. It was not impressed by the numbers of subscribers to such systems, by the nature of those systems themselves or by their promise of success. Although there were over 2 million subscribers to cable systems, the systems were limited in capacity and also out-dated. The Technical Advisory Committee 1972[10], had pointed out that about 60 per cent of television relay systems were based on the High Frequency multi-pair system and only 40 per cent on the more advanced co-axial cable system. Neither system could offer more than half-a-dozen televison channels. These factors confirmed the Committee's view that cable systems ought to remain as local distribution systems only. It could not see cable systems surviving in an era of universal coverage and it did not believe that cable could offer anything new or worthwhile. Though pay-TV was probably 'the best financial proposition' for the relay operators:

from what we saw in North America we did not

conclude that the more channels a viewer could switch to the greater the choice ...what (cable) did was to distribute material from broadcasting organisations, feature films and some live sport. It was therefore a ravenous parasite. [11]

Another consideration for the Committee was that cable systems had failed to develop significantly in the various experiments permitted in the previous decade. The experimental subscription television services in Sheffield and London in 1968 were financial disasters and the community television experiments of 1972 and 1976 fared no better. In this latter period, the Conservative government had given permission to 5 cable system operators to carry a community programme channel for an unlimited period of time. With no signs of the government relaxing its regulation so as to permit either advertising on the community channel (permission was eventually granted in 1975, too late to be of any help) or some form of subscription television to offset the cost of the community service and so boost cable's fortunes, the community channels did not prove to be financially viable and they were terminated within 3 to 4 years. [12]

Finally, since cable was perceived as a national distribution system there was little point in recommending minor developments. The problem here was that the national system would require many years to develop, would need to be publicly funded and directed and would be extremely costly. And as the recession deepened it was unlikely that any body would recommend such vast sums of expenditure; a national system was effectively out of reach.

Cable television systems in the 1970s were then essentially no different from the radio relay systems of the 1920s. The regulatory framework, shoring up a by now mythologised version of 'public service broadcasting' - who could, after all, now tell the difference between the BBC and the ITV system - had corralled them neatly and safely into the recesses of the broadcasting system. But within a few years, cable was at the beginning of an expansionist and almost revolutionary phase. How did this reversal of fortunes come about and what were its likely consequences? Those issues are explored in the next section.

BROADCASTING, CABLE AND THE CONSERVATIVE GOVERNMENT, 1979 TO 1984

The Conservative government's victory in the general election of 1979 marks the turning point for cable's fortunes in Britain. The Government's preference for laissez-faire market economics, denationalisation (or privatisation) and a penchant for private entrepreneurial activity that was likely to regenerate and rekindle Britain's flagging industrial power heralded a change in British political and economic life.

Such a radical approach undoubtedly favoured private enterprise and it was not long after the election that the first fruits of its victory could be enjoyed. In the sphere of broadcasting one could see this in two inter-linked processes, each of which is connected in some way to the work of the Advisory Council for the Advancement of Research and Development (ACARD): one concerns the area of broadcasting policy and regulations, the other focuses on the government's commitment to industrial change and development.

Broadcasting Policy

Thatcher's government has lived up to the tradition of Conservative governments introducing major changes in Britain's broadcasting structures. Just as earlier governments had set up the commercial broadcasting network and BBC 2, the Thatcher government has presided over the inauguration of Channel 4.

But in the first few years of its life, the government did not apply its reforming zeal to the field of cable. The Home Secretary's (then W.Whitelaw) approach to cable provided a continuity in policy which could be traced back for many decades. Broadcasting was still something to be cherished and protected. Thus, Whitelaw's promise to the Cable Television Association in November 1979 of consultations to explore 'the conditions in which subscription TV might be allowed to go forward' was made in his (government's?) belief that 'cable TV has an important role to play in a broadcasting system which we want to preserve and develop'.[13] A year later he announced his intentions to consider applications from existing cable television licensees to run pay-TV services. There would be a dozen 'pilot schemes' designed 'to determine the appropriate regulatory framework within which cable might develop'.[14]

The traditional, Home Office inspired, approach to
broadcasting, cable and its regulation was clearly
evident in these statements. These suggested a
lengthy process of consultations, reports and
discussions. It was an established approach and not
greatly dissimilar from that of the outgoing Labour
government. In the latter's response to the Annan
Committee, it too accepted the need for experimentation with pay-TV; 'provisions' it noted 'will
...be made in the new legislation to enable pilot
schemes of pay-TV to be authorised subject to
careful regulation to guard against the possible
damaging effects which pay-TV might have on
television as a whole...'.[15]
    This continuity in thought and practice,
united in its acceptance of changes of an
incremental and marginal kind, was rudely broken by
the growing political and industrial popularity of
Information Technology. At first, this new current
of thought worked in parallel with the Home
Office's policy-making cycle [16] but it was soon to
dominate all other considerations. So much so that
the 'pilot schemes' became anachronisms and, more
crucially, the Department of Trade and Industry
gained a large measure of influence over cable
matters and, hence, broadcasting related issues.

Information Technology (IT)
Interest in information technology - generally, the
interconnection between telecommunications and
computers - predates the existence of the
Conservative government by many years. ACARD, for
example, was set up in 1976 by the Labour
government. Nonetheless, it was a Conservative
government which grasped some of the opportunities
it presented. This is best illustrated by an
examination of ACARD's influence on the development
of cable in Britain.
    In September 1980, the Council published one
of a series of reports on 'the implications of the
rapid developments taking place in microelectronic
technology' and it made a number of 'proposals to
stimulate the use of this technology in United
Kingdom industry'. This report, 'Technological
Change'[17] identified IT as possibly the area of
application with the greatest potential for
creating employment and for generating valuable
exports.
    The Council subsequently set up a working
party - consisting in the main of business and
industrial interests - to 'identify the likely

directions of development'.[18] Its recommendations
in effect called upon the Government to co-ordinate
its own, and public, efforts in this area and to
encourage industry generally to explore information
technology and its applications. Though the report
does not specifically call for the introduction of
a cable network per se, it favoured the development
and exploitation of all microelectronic systems
which could handle, store and process information.
    ACARD's calls for action found a responsive
chord in a government committed to radical
policies. Within 6 months of the report's
publication, a Minister was appointed with
responsibility for Information Technology within
the Department of Trade and Industry. This was in
line with the report's thinking. Kenneth Baker, the
new Minister, was known to be a fervent advocate of
IT and was soon to champion its cause. The
government also designated 1982 as IT year and it
subsequently focused on IT as a favourite candidate
for introducing industrial growth and renewal in
Britain. Again, very much in the spirit of the
ACARD report. As Thatcher remarked in July 1981,
'The government fully recognises the importance of
information technology for the future industrial
and commercial success of the UK and the central
role that the government must play in promoting its
development and application'.[19]
    In order to pursue these aims, an IT Advisory
Panel (ITAP) and an IT Unit were set up within the
Cabinet Office. The former was to advise on IT
policies and strategies and the latter was to give
an overall coherence to the government's efforts in
this area. The significance of this approach to IT
can be seen in the placing of both the Panel and
the Unit in the Cabinet Office and not in Civil
Service departments as would have usually been the
case. This not only short-circuited the usual
processes of inquiry and decision-making, but it
also seemed to favour those who would encourage a
policy of regeneration which directly, and
indirectly, benefitted their respective industries.
ITAP's membership included, for example, the
Managing Director of Rediffusion (Britain's largest
single cable system operator and a major electronic
and communication enterprise; in October 1984 it
was taken over by Pergamon Press, a part of
R.Maxwell's communications empire), the Managing
Director of Mullard (a major electronics firm) and
assorted banking and computing executives.[20] A
decision in favour of cable technology would

clearly be advantageous to all these sectors involving as they do the storage and transfer of information and entertainment. As ITAP was to observe in its report, 'Cable Systems', published in February 1982 'the main role of cable systems eventually will be the delivery of many information,financial and other services to the home, and the joining of businesses and homes by high capacity data links'.[21]

The ITAP Report

But the report, a mere 54 pages, is a major turning point for cable in Britain for other, equally important, reasons. Not only did it publicly encourage the speedy development of cable systems and services - 'a delayed decision' it claimed' is the same as a negative decision'[22] - it also seemed to articulate the government's views on the prospect and promise of this technological revolution. As Baker, the Minister for Information Technology, remarked in a speech made not long after the report's publication:

> We are pressing ahead very rapidly at the moment with cable television, hoping to lay down in this country, beginning next year, the start of a totally interactive cable network....Laying down that cable television network will be as important as the laying down of the railway network in Victorian England....'[23]

In the report, one can also find the main strands of what was to become the government's policy on cable television. Five major points stand out. Firstly, there was a commitment to the private funding of cable systems as against either a publicly funded national development or one that gave British Telecom (the PTT) a major role in the development of the network. ITAP did acknowledge, however, that private funding would not be attracted by the prospect of the 'future communications system'. 'The initial financing of cable systems will depend...upon estimates of the revenue from additional popular programming channels'.[24] This was the crux of the 'entertainment-led' policy: popular programming would eventually pull through the other components of the future communications system.

The consequences of this position - and it is one that the government has accepted - are significant. Not only does it negate any possibility of a centralised, government directed and publicly funded strategy but it puts the emphasis on privately led development in the hope that the latter will lead to the future communications network. Whether independent local initiatives can produce the integrated, interactive network that the government has been so keen to publicise is a moot point.

But this strategy of private funding was only feasible if the restrictions on the services that can be carried on cable systems are removed; if, in other words, 'the government lifts the present constraints on the programmes that may be distributed by cable operators and allows a full range of programmes and services to be provided'.[25]

Secondly, ITAP recommended that the government should announce, by mid-1982, that is, at very short notice, the broad outlines of its future policy towards cable and that that policy should be to 'license new systems conforming to set technical standards but without the present restrictions on programmes....under existing legislation and administrative arrangements'.[26] Thirdly, that the government should review the implications of cable for broadcasting and also 'consider the need for a new statutory body....for cable systems'.[27]

Fourthly, although ITAP did not wish to 'prejudice commercial operations' by setting rigid technical standards, its recommendations favoured technologically advanced, switched systems capable of 'incremental expansion beyond a defined minimum number of channels (perhaps 30) without disturbance to the final distribution network'.[28]

Finally, the Panel also recommended that the government approve the early start of DBS as a measure to help cable systems. This recommendation was in fact implemented just before the report was made public though the original starting date for DBS has been put back from 1986 to 1988. There have also been some major changes in the organisational structure of the DBS enterprise.

Following the publication of the ITAP report, developments took place at a fairly rapid pace. The Hunt Committee was set up to examine the implications of cable for broadcasting and to make recommendations about programming and the regulatory framework. In line with the plea for speedy action, it reported back in September 1982.[29] In April 1983, the government published its White Paper on 'The Development of Cable Systems and Services'[30] and this confirmed many of the recommendations made at earlier stages. It adopted the market/entertainment-led expansion policy; there was to be a flexible and liberalised approach to cable and its services; it favoured technologically advanced broadband multi-channel cable systems; a new Cable Authority would be set up to allocate future franchise applications and to supervise and oversee the operation of cable systems and, most importantly, it suggested that some franchises would be granted prior to the new Authority coming into existence.

After the White Paper had been debated and approved by Parliament, the Home Office and the Department of Trade and Industry published their joint 'Guidance Note' for prospective applicants in July 1983. These proposed the (interim) licensing of 'a limited number (maximum 12) of cable systems as pilot projects' and also the licensing of 'existing cable operators to offer additional programme services.'[31] In both cases, this process would precede the setting up of the new Authority. The decision to offer two types of licences was predicated on the need to encourage new developments and, at the same time, to meet many of the needs and demands of existing cable system operators. As a consequence, there would be some major differences - in size, capability, duration of the licence -between these two groups of cable operators.

Nonetheless, and despite the many contradictions that are apparant in the government's approach, it has effectively brought about some remarkable changes in the face of British broadcasting. It has made provisions for the widespread, privately funded, development of cable systems and, unlike Whitelaw's 'pilot schemes', these developments would be of a long term and permanant nature. Such changes also foreshadowed the establishment of rivals to the existing broadcasting authorities with a substantial degree of autonomy regarding what they are able to carry on their systems. Cable operators will have none of the 'obligations' of public service broadcasters, except perhaps those of ensuring that all programmes were decent and fair.

Two other changes are worth noting. Firstly, the government has forced the Home Office, the traditional centre for broadcasting affairs, and the Department of Trade and Industry, with its new acquired interest in IT, to work together - if not always amicably - 'to catch the tide of technological development while at the same time securing an

orderly revolution'.[32] Henceforth, matters related
to cable would be dealt with by both departments.

Secondly, and perhaps most critically, the
government has short-circuited the policy-making
process and the public debate on the grounds that
the pace of change did not permit lengthy
discussions. It has taken less than three years to
achieve all this when, in contrast, it took nearly
a decade to bring about the development of the
fourth channel.

To a critic, none of the above points are
particularly worthwhile. In Peter Fiddick's eyes 'a
laudiable policy for industrial regeneration,
employment and exports (where these might have
existed) has turned out to be a short-dash'.[33]
Others have similarly argued that the whole
strategy was founded on the ITAP report which was
'misleading' and 'based on wishful and selective
reading of the American experience'.[34] Still others
have contributed their private, and public,
thoughts on the disjunction between the initial
promise and the impending reality of the situation:
there have been doubts cast on ITAP's estimates of
the growth potential of cable in the next decade,
on whether there is sufficient private funding to
bring about even a modest growth, on the financial
viability and profitability of such growth, on the
employment prospects offered by cable development
in Britain and even on the export prospects of
cable technology.[35] Finally, it is very possible
that cable television systems will not find it easy
to win subscribers in a nation noted for its high
take-up of video cassette recorders. It is
estimated that by the end of 1984, 4 out of every
ten homes will have access to a VCR and that, as a
result, cable operators will not find a ready
market for their wares since the public already has
easy access to a wide range of entertainment
material. Early results from some cable operators
have tended to support this view though the
situation is changing slowly.

Some of these concerns have attracted the
attention of the Government and in May 1984 it
referred the whole issue of cable developments to
the Economist Intelligence Unit for a report on the
current situation, the difficulties and some of the
obstacles that have emerged since those early days
of optimism.[36]

These criticisms and reappraisals - however
valid - are now academic. Cable's immediate
development is assured under the present legislative
structure and as indicated in the Cable and

Broadcasting Bill which became law in July of 1984. Many developments are already under way: eleven (not 12) pilot project licences were awarded in November 1983 and in December 1983 the Home Secretary also announced his approval to license applications from existing cable operators to run additional programme services. However, the longer term developments are difficult to discern and much will depend on the experiences of those presently running 'upgraded systems' and of those operators who are currently setting up the proposed 11 cable projects.

Despite the many reservations one might have about the future progress and viability of cable television in Britain, it is important to stress that in bringing about these changes the government has fulfilled some of the cable industry's long standing demands. Historically, cable operators have always desired the opportunity to supply their subscribers with services other than were ordinarily available. This was partly a response to some of the network's unused capacity but it was mainly based on a belief that the customer should have the right to choose whatever she/he wished from a range of services. This latter belief was premised on economic considerations: the operator would supply what the subscriber wanted and was willing to pay for. Indeed, the 'plan for consumer choice' provided the central strategy in the industry's previous concerted attempts to get changes introduced in the regulations that affected their systems and services.

The Cable Television Association's document, 'A plan for consumer choice', well illustrated the nature of these demands. It envisaged the build-up of cable television services, based on existing networks, to include extra channels according to demand. It observed that the 'Freedom to operate on the basis of a normal marketing relationship between supplier and consumer would open doors to a new era in neighbourhood communication, with widespread benefits to life and leisure'.[37]

The Association further claimed that such a plan could become reality overnight for many towns in Britain - in 1972 there were 2778 systems covering about 13% of television households - provided that the restrictions on operators were lifted. Again, the liberalisation of policies was seen as crucial for the future development of cable in Britain; in practice, however, the operators were restricted by their licences and so could not exploit their systems to the full. Such exploitation has, in 1984/85 a familiar ring about it: the 1973 plan included film channels, children's channels, sports channels, news channels, local channels and the like.

That plan, and other attempts at liberalisation, came to nothing. A decade later, it is effectively being revived and as cable television gradually spreads in Britain, it must be remembered that it is the entertainment side which will be exploited first. Additional, interactive type, services will be part of a long term strategy of technological development and marketing of broadband cable systems. Unfortunately, by making technological development dependent on the success of entertainment on cable it may be that certain aspects may have to be sacrificed since what may be required to run entertainment systems may not match the needs of technologically advanced systems.

CABLE TELEVISION IN THE 1980s

The Pilot Projects
By far the most important aspect of the government's industrial strategy towards IT development was its readiness to license a limited number of cable pilot projects 'in order not to lose the momentum which (had) already been created'. These projects were to be licensed prior to the creation of the proposed Cable Authority and were thus to provide a real indication of the government's intentions, and commitment to cable and IT. The licences awarded were of an 'interim' nature, though, in view of the fact that the terms and conditions might be modified as a consequence of changes made by Parliament to both the Cable and Broadcasting Bill and the Telecommunications Act, 1984, and of decisions which would fall within the discretion of the proposed Authority.

The Guidance Note for potential applicants, produced jointly by the Home Office and the Department of Trade and Industry, set out fairly clearly the government's thinking. It would award up to 12 interim licences to those applicants who were most likely to provide the sort of telecommunications infrastructure and services that fully displayed cable's potential. Priority would be given to 'those proposals which offer the most positive contribution of the application of advanced technology and which provide a comprehensive range of programme services and the capability for interactive services'[38]

A licensed system would cover 'a maximum of around 100,000 homes in an identifiable and self-contained community'. Although this figure is substantially lower than the Hunt Inquiry's recommendation of a 500,000 maximum,[39] the intention here, as in Hunt, was to retain cable as a local system. Since the award of the licences in November 1983, however, some systems have had their maximum increased up to about 130,000 homes.

There were to be specific, albeit minimal conditions, concerning the programme services to be made available on the pilot projects. The 30 channel systems would have to carry all the existing broadcasting services plus the proposed DBS services. This was the so-called 'must carry' rule. In all other respects, the operators were free to carry whatever they desired provided that certain conditions were met. For example, there was to be no adult channel, advertising was to conform to commercial television regulations, 'a proper proportion' (sic) of material shown was to come from Britain and the EEC and pay-per-view and sponsorship would not be permitted prior to the Authority coming into existence.

Despite the short notice given - there were only 6 weeks between the issue of the Guidance Note and the closing date of 31 August, 1983 - 37 applications were received and eventually 11 were chosen by the Economist Informatics Unit. This non-governmental body was allocated the task of examining proposals and selecting the winners. Many of the applications had come from consortia of business and media interests set up with the specific task of exploring and exploiting cable developments. As Table 4.1 shows, many of the 11 successful applicants are of this nature. Of these 11, 8 have decided to adopt switched systems and others have retained the tree and branch configuration. In practice, though, all will employ some form of hybrid system developed either indigenously or adapted from the United States industry. Furthermore, because it will take another two to three years to perfect the switched technology so desired by the Department of Trade and Industry, it is highly likely that the projects will adopt a system of developmental stages introducing the new technologies as, and when, they appear. Aberdeen Cablevision, for example, proposes to install a tree and branch system in the first place although it will be laid

Cable Television in Great Britain

in a star configuration so that it will be
relatively easy to upgrade the system to a mini-hub
switch system.[40] In at least 5 cases, the
construction of the network will be carried out by
British Telecom while other operators have chosen
such companies as GEC-Delta Kabel, Cabletime,
STC-Texscan. However, as costs continue to escalate
these choices may be subject to change. To date,
some changes have already taken place though the
licensees will still be obliged to install advanced
broadband systems in line with the government's
original intentions.

Table 4.1: Franchises Awarded in 1983

Organisation	Major Shareholders
Aberdeen Cable	Industrial & Commercial Finance Corp., BT, American TV and Communications.
Cabletel Communications (London area)	Ladbroke, Comcast Corp., Legal and General PLC.
Coventry Cable	Thorn EMI, DT.
Swindon Cable	Thorn EMI.
Ulster Cablevision	BT, Standard Telephones and Cables, Thorn EMI, Ulster TV.
Clyde Cablevision (Glasgow area)	Industrial & Commercial Finance Corp., Murray Clydesdale Investments, Mirror Group Newspapers.
Croydon Cable (London area)	Balfour Beattie, Cablevision Int., Racal Oak, Wates Builders, Croydon Advertiser.
Merseyside Cablevision	Pilkington Bros., Virgin, BT, BICC, Pergamon Press/BPCC.
Guildford	originally Rediffusion, now Pergamon Press. Plans are to be resubmitted.
Westminster Cable (London area)	Kleinwort Benson, Plessey, British Information Technology, BT, AT & C.
Windsor TV	CIN Industrial Investments, GEC.

It goes without saying that the commitment to
advanced technology has a high price attached to
it. Each project will cost around £30 to £40

million and to compensate for this heavy investment programme, the successful applicants were initially awarded a 12 year programme licence and a 20 year telecommunications licence. It is worth emphasising at this stage that operators of broadband cable systems in Britain actually require two types of licences. For the provision of television programme services, they require a licence from, at present, the Home Office; in order to comply with technical and other regulatory provisions regarding the delivery of telecommunications services, they also require a licence from the Department of Trade and Industry. In future, these licences will be awarded by the Cable Authority in consultation with both the present regulatory departments.

The separate identities of cable - as telecommunications and as television - have surfaced at many points: in the Guidance Note, in the requirement of two licences, in the involvement of two quite separate and ideologically distinct government departments. All this has had a considerable impact on those directly involved in contemporary cable developments. Also, awarding licences in an atmosphere of great interest in IT - hence the emphasis on broadband systems - downgraded the real difficulties of the cable television industry. Questions of cost, programming, marketing and profitability appeared secondary to a cabling 'at all costs' strategy. This was further aggravated by a frenetic franchising process. As one consultant observed 'are we in danger of creating a situation where franchise bidders are committing themselves to technology which is not ready, and fully costed, and to services for which the markets are not even partly proven'?[41]

Recent events have highlighted other difficulties that can be linked to the policy of speedy development. Successful applicants had to wait many months for their licences and contracts and this has slowed down progress considerably. But the greatest blow to the cable television industry was, however, of a different order. In the Budget of March 1984, it was announced that capital allowances would be phased out from 1986. Expenditure on plant, machinery and buildings would no longer be allowed against tax and though there would be a gradual phasing out of all these allowances, all the 11 franchise holders had to review their expenditure plans. Amid rumours of difficulties, there was also a sense of great disappointment: economic policy objectives over-ruled one of the Department of Trade and Industry's favourite IT projects. The precise effects of these changes are unknown though it is clear that the turnaround to profitability has probably been put back a number of years.[42] To compensate for the effects of these changes, pilot project licences were extended by a period of three years.

So, while 1984 was then generally seen as a depressing year for the cable industry, there are signs that 1985 may be equally worrying. As of January 1985, only 1 pilot project is in operation and it covers only a minute fraction of the potential households in its franchise area. This lack of progress by the industry has worried both politicians and cable operators. Certainly, the optimism of 1982 and 1983 has almost completely vanished as licensees find it increasingly difficult to finance their embryonic operations. Amidst talk of possible withdrawals and reconsiderations of initial plans, it is becoming clear that the commitment to advanced technology is proving too costly and that few, if any, financial investors are so convinced of cable's future growth and profitability as to provide the necessary venture capital to make it a success. It may be that the commitment to advanced technology will be shelved so as to give operators a chance to start building their networks. Similar difficulties have been encountered by the DBS project and it is not at all clear whether it will be operational before 1988 at the earliest.

Upgraded Systems

While most of cable's exciting developments are unlikely to be fully operational before 1986, the government's willingness to grant licences to existing cable television systems' operators has permitted some innovation in television programme provision to take place immediately. Such licences were granted to operators who wished to 'provide programme services additional to those of the BBC and IBA over their existing relay sytems'.[43] As these conditions probably applied to a majority of Britain's cable operators, it enabled them to benefit from the government's liberalisation of the conditions surrounding the provisions of programme services without incurring major developmental costs.

Cable operators were once again, as in previous 'pilot schemes', being offered the opportunity of introducing a whole range of pay-TV services. But since existing systems were mainly of a limited capacity, mainly 4 to 6 channel systems, the government imposed certain conditions to ensure that the broadcasting services did not suffer detrimentally from the new licencing procedures. The 'must carry' rule would therefore not apply to limited capacity systems where arrangements were made for subscribers to receive, by alternative means, the BBC and IBA services. One way of doing this would be to supply aerials to households so releasing the cable network from carrying the broadcast services. Systems of greater capacity would still have to comply with the 'must carry' rule but were otherwise free to offer any number of additional services up to the existing capacity of each individual system.

The adoption of this strategy has effectively prolonged the lifetime of a rather out dated technology. But it does have some positive merits. It commits cable operators to cable systems and encourages them to exploit them; it encourages them to sell new additional programme services to subscribers and, finally, it provides a real testing ground for the demand for the services that cable may be able to provide. As always, the new additional services would have to conform to existing regulations concerning taste and decency, impartiality and fairness and advertising content. Operators, however, would not be permitted to carry certain national events, e.g. Wimbledon tennis, on an exclusive basis.

Licences for 'upgraded' systems were awarded 'in the first instance' until 31 July 1986 and there were no guarantees that extensions would be granted. The main reason for the short duration of the licence was that the government did not wish to prevent new (broadband) cable projects from covering the same area in future years. Thus, the licence gave existing operators a period of grace prior to another, and perhaps major, round of competitive bidding. After 1986, though, the bidding would be for the right to build broadband cable systems. In this way, no area would be permanently excluded from the prospect of the cable revolution.

At present, there are some 11 organisations licenced under these provisions and some operators will operate in more than one area. Rediffusion (now part of Pergamon Press) will operate in 53 areas, Radio Rentals in 8, British Telecom in 3 areas. An early casuality amongst these has been the Visionhire networks; its withdrawal from several areas in October 1984 only confirmed the belief that the industry was in a depression and that it had many real obstacles - mainly financial - to overcome. All existing operators, however, intend to provide a range of new television programme services. It is estimated that by 1986, these systems may pass about 2 million homes. Take-up of these services has so far been generally considered poor though there are signs that this is changing.

INTO THE CABLE ERA: CONTROLS AND CONTENT

After a lengthy delay, the government announced the setting up of the Cable Authority in November 1984. As yet, it has made few pronouncements though its general duties will be to oversee the cable television sector. Its functions will be to decide on future applications for licences and to exercise a measure of oversight - 'a light regulatory touch'[44] - over the cable operators and their systems It has already announced its intention to advertise another 5 cable franchises even though the details of its work have yet to be finalised. There are, however, a number of broad guidelines that it will attempt to observe.

In awarding future licences it will have to ensure that the applications meet certain technical requirements as set out by the new Office of Telecommunications (OFTEL). The Authority will also have to see that certain groups - bodies outside the EEC, media interests, religious and political groups and local authorities - do not have shareholdings in the applicant body to an extent deemed 'adverse to the public interest'.

Once a licence is awarded, the cable operator will be able to carry any television programmes or additional services that she/he wishes to subject to some very standard conditions, such as, matters of taste, decency, fairness, maximum advertising time permitted on television channels etc..'Adult' programmes will not be permitted though pay-per-view and sponsorship of programmes will be once the Authority is in place. Also, the Authority will have to see that a 'proper proportion', of programmes are of British or EEC origin; at present, the BBC and IBA operate a 14% quota on imported material.[45]

In one sense, the Authority will be granting operators a monopoly. It is not clear on what grounds it can withdraw licences and it is unlikely

123

that it would ever do so given the vast sums that operators will have to invest. It is also uncertain whether the Authority will be able to force or require operators to do that which they do not desire on grounds of cost. For example, it can only encourage operators to carry a community service or to lease or 'dedicate' certain channels to groups. Since the question of the viability of these services and the exercise of editorial control over these services have yet to be worked out, the prospect of new innovations, e.g. in news, minority or fringe group services, is somewhat dimmed.

In practice, then, the Authority will establish and supervise a system of 'broadcasting' that is very different to the one that already exists. While the BBC, for instance, has to provide a range of services, cable operators will only be guided by commercial considerations. This duality will aggravate the Authority's work as it tries to exert control over its charges so as to balance requirements of decency and quality, demands for alternative services and market forces - factors over which it has no power.

But the work of the Authority will not be as onerous as the above suggests for it is likely that the range of services that it will have to oversee will be fairly narrow and predictable. In the first instance, the interactive services of tele-banking and tele-shopping are a long way off and so not matters of immediate concern. In any case, their provision will depend on marketing strategies and the service providers' willingness to pay for them rather than of regulatory fiat. Secondly, and as current experience shows, the types of television programme services that it will have to supervise will present few major problems. Films, sport and general entertainment are not matters of controversy although it is possible that a 'news' service might cause a bit of a stir given the general critique of news content in British broadcasting over the last 2 decades.

As Table 4.2 shows, the organisations now supplying additional programme services are working with a limited menu. It is likely that new programme services will be introduced in time to meet the inauguration of the multi-channel systems but which proposed services will survive beyond the planning stage is difficult to predict.

These programme services display the usual characteristics of the new cable age. The programmes are provided by organisations which are

not always separate from the licensees and the
programme services are delivered to the cable
operators via satellite links. In Britain both
Intelsat V and ECS-1 are used by these services.
The existing programme services are currently
available on most of the newly licensed upgraded
cable systems and operators are charging their
subscribers a basic fee for the non-premium
services and an extra fee for the film channels.
This usually works out at about £5 for the basic
service and £8 for the premium services. No
upgraded system is currently carrying more than one
premium service.

Table 4.2: Existing, and Proposed, New Programme Services

Organisation	Type of Service	Ownership
Sky Channel	general entertainment	Satellite TV Ltd.
Music Box	music service	Thorn EMI Screen Entertainment, Virgin Records Yorkshire TV.
Screen Sport	sport	R.Kennedy,ESPN,ABC Video Enterprises
TEN	movie-channel	United Cable Progs. (Pergamon Press, MGM/UA Rank,Paramount,Universal).
Premiere	movie-channel	Thorn EMI Screen Entertainment, Columbia Pictures, HBO,Warner,Showtime/Movie Channel, 20th Century Fox.
The Children's Channel	childrens channel	Thames TV,Thorn EMI, Pergamon Press.

Some Proposed Services	
The Arts Channel	a cultural service
Key Channel	a channel for sponsored material
Spectrum	a channel for sponsored material
The Games' Channel	a video games channel owned by W.H.Smith
Gamestar	a video games channel from British Telecom
A News Channel	
A 'Lifestyle' channel	

Operators of the new 30 channel broadband systems are hoping to make use of all the available services including those which require interactive facilities. Thus, their plans go beyond merely supplying a new range of television output and include proposals for security systems, tele-shopping and tele-banking, betting facilities, educational programmes and local and community services. Some proposals also include the prospect of telephonic services though there are grave doubts as to the feasibility of this service[46] or indeed the viability of any other of the services mentioned above.

So whilst the future pattern of available programmes is as yet uncertain, it is becoming clear that the British scene will be heavily influenced by American interests and by existing programme providers, e.g. commercial television companies. Little new blood or money has been injected into the programme production side of the cable revolution: the costs of making and distributing material are proving prohibitive and future programme suppliers will have to find a way of producing material at a fraction of present costs if they are to find cable operators as customers.[47]

The drive all round to keep costs down has put the emphasis on the existing and established interests, as Table 4.2 indicates. There is also pressure to reach the largest possible audience and this may push programme providers to launch European DBS, rather than UK only, services. For example, a cultural channel - by definition, a minority channel - may be financially viable only within the European framework. So, as programme providers link up separate cable systems in some sort of national grid and nations with other nations, the room for regional and even local services becomes smaller and smaller. Cable, instead of providing the much heralded community communications may end up working in the opposite direction.

THE IMPACT OF CABLE TELEVISION ON BROADCASTING

The potential damage that cable television can inflict on a structure of broadcasting founded on 'public service' principles has, for long, been of concern to many. Even in the early days of radio relay such concerns were frequently voiced. The principle that Reith, the BBC's first Director

General, was trying to uphold was one that emphasised high quality broadcasting to the public at large with no discrimination as to income and class. But Reith understood that to strive for this goal one had to exercise a large measure of control over the structure and content of broadcasting. In the case of the BBC, this derived from its monopoly over broadcasting, its guaranteed income from the licence fee and a high moral ideal.[48]

Such conditions are not those of a commercial organisation. Without the obligations of 'public service' - and the conditions which permitted their pursuit - a commercial organisation would be forced to favour the most popular, the cheapest and therefore the most profitable fare regardless of its cultural merit.

Participants in recent cable debates have employed more sophisticated versions of this argument but, in essence, their concern can be likened to those of Reith. As the BBC remarked in its submission to the Hunt Committee, cable will erode and undermine public service broadcasting and be 'socially divisive, sacrifice hard-won programme standards and coarsen a public taste which has been painstakingly developed by public service broadcasting'.[49]

In principle, it may be possible to justify such a view. In practice, the changes that will come about as a direct result of cable will depend greatly on its popularity and penetration in Britain. At the present rate of progress, it may be that by 1986 - when, and if, the 11 pilot projects are fully operational - between 3 and 4 million households will be passed by both old and new cable systems. This represents about 16 to 21 per cent of Britain's 19 million homes. If one assumes that the penetration level will be in the range of 30 to 40 per cent, then the total number of subscribers will be in the region of 1 to 2 million. It must be remembered though that only a fraction of these will be connected to the new broadband systems. By 1990, that figure is likely to be higher though it will depend on the rate at which new broadband systems come into operation and older ones close down. Both these factors will themselves be dependent on the projected profitability of cable. Despite the recent setbacks for the cable industry, there does not appear to be a shortage of organisations ready to apply for cable operators licences in the next round of applications which is expected to take place sometime in early 1985. More interestingly, it is very likely that the 'upgraded' licensees will be allowed to continue to operate past July 1986. So, while cable's growth is assured, the issue is the rate at which it will grow.

Optimistic forecasts for 1995, ten years hence, suggest that 50 per cent of UK households will be passed by cable. At a penetration rate of 40 per cent, this produces about 5 million cable subscribers; a more realistic penetration rate of about 30 per cent suggests that there will only be about 4.5 million subscribers in all. In practice, these figures are subject to wide variation and the recent problems of the industry have further affected the initial projection by reducing the slope of the growth curve.

Even the more optimistic figures, however, indicate that in the next decade cable will still be of 'minority' appeal. At this level, it is difficult to see it as a deadly rival to the existing services. Nor does it make DBS - its other rival for the provision of additional services - redundant overnight. Admittedly, the history of DBS in Britain has been fraught with problems and delays. But its ability to deliver a European market makes it ideal for the provision of certain programme services which may not be profitable in a British market alone. A good example of such a service is a cultural channel.

Cable's impact, then, cannot be quantified with any precision. As the industry battles to survive, grave doubts are again being expressed over the whole nature of the government's policies towards cable. These policies have forced operators to commit themselves to a costly and unproven technology without having any recourse to financial aid from the government. Furthermore, the government's free market approach has forced it to ignore pleas for help. While this may be justified politically, it does raise many issues about the need for a clear and far-sighted view of technological change - a view which does not appear to exist.

The ups and downs of current developments have tended to give a sense of unreality to present discussions. It becomes an act of bravery to discuss cable as the technology of the future yet it is an act of dispondancy to dismiss it. All signs point to a rather slow growth and so the challenge of cable may still be some way off.

But, cable has undoubtedly had an important impact on thinking about the nature of the broadcasting system generally. In this sense, cable does offer a real challenge to the existing broadcasting services since it undermines what were once certainties. It is unlikely that the existing duopoly will remain unaffected by cable television and some commercial television organisations have already made provisions to supply cable systems and so develop a new, and interesting policy, of co-existence. Even though the BBC has so far refused to make provisions for cable programmes - it does, after all, control a vast library of material - the onset of cable has exercised the minds of many of its managers. In an increasingly competitive media environment, no organisation can afford to ignore the prospect of significant changes both in the range of television programmes now available to the public and in the new approach to the viewer which this new range exemplifies.

For those willing to consider a policy of co-existence an important issue is the point at which cable television begins to erode and detrimentally affect the nature of the BBC and ITV system itself. If cable television remains a 'minority' service then its impact will be small though not insignificant; if take-up proves to be high then that impact will be of a major kind. Much will also depend on whether the funding structures of the two existing broadcasting Authorities are, or are not, at risk. If they are not, then competition from cable television may be healthy; if funding is at risk, for example, by pegging the BBC licence fee, affecting the ITV companies advertising rates or diminishing the BBC's status as the national force of broadcasting, then the challenge from cable may be somewhat for the worst as its effects impinge on the production of programmes. It is not that such pressures on finite resources do not already exist and are being felt by broadcasters particularly within the licence funded BBC but that cable introduces more, and possibly severe, competition at a time when such pressure is enormous.

None of these reasons are, in themselves, sufficient arguments against the introduction of cable television or indeed any other broadcasting service. For, despite the admirable record of quality and consistency in British broadcasting, there has always been much to criticise. Britain has had its monopoly, its quiz shows, soap operas and repeat programmes; there have also been many occasions when the television companies have not delivered what they had promised. Furthermore, the last three decades have seen an expansion in the broadcasting services (in both radio and television) which has, in part, reflected a changing social and political context. Few would, for example, wish to return to the BBC monopoly or to television without Channel Four. In change, then, there is both good and bad and Britain has been lucky enough to ensure that there is more of the former than of the latter.

Why there should be no further change in British broadcasting may then be the central question in the cable television debate. One reason could be that it could detrimentally affect the programming on BBC and ITV. The case for this is not fully proven, though there are obvious dangers. To avoid this danger, one may need to guarantee the security of the existing services by guaranteeing, for example, the BBC its licence fee. Such an approach would call for a review of all the broadcasting services and the development of a coherent policy towards them. It is an approach that favours an integration of services rather than outright competition. However, such a review should not presume that new services ought not to develop; restrictions on new services of national and even local character have often appeared bureaucratic and censorious.

A more powerful reason for not permitting wholesale cable television developments is, we suggest, that the new services will neither provide different services nor extend the range of control and ownership. An exploration of the ownership structure of both cable operators and programme providers demonstrates how narrow their base is. Existing interests dominate all areas.

The cable revolution will then be driven forwards by those already committed, financially and institutionally, to the present. They will benefit from what it can bring: new tele-banking and tele-shopping services as a way of reducing manpower needs; premium films, sports and children's programmes as a way of achieving profitability. Their moral, social or public responsibilities will be dwarfed by the economic logic of their organisations.

For the future, there is one issue that has not received much comment. If the nature of the cable revolution has already been determined and the usual institutional players are now occupying the most favourable places, what happens if, or when, their plans do not measure up to the full potential of cable television and cable tele-communications? If, in other words, the economic logic does not touch upon the social and political benefits that broadband systems can deliver. Will the speed at which cable developments had been pursued proved worthwhile? Will the policy to favour private developments and not national ones have proved unwise? Will the 'wired society' be dismissed as an illusion rather than perhaps an illusion if developed in private hands? Finally, will the public, in whose name so much has been promised, be able to reclaim the cable revolution for itself and for a better society?

The Author would like to thank the Nuffield Foundation, London for assistance in financing the research on which this chapter is based.

NOTES

1. BBC (1935), Submission to the Ullswater Committee 1935, HMSO, London, Paper 68.

2. R.Negrine (1984), 'From Radio Relay to Cable Television: the British experience', The Historical Journal of Film, Radio and Television, Vol. 4, No.1.

3. A.Briggs (1965), The Golden Age of Wireless, Oxford University Press, London.

4. White Paper on Broadcasting (1978), Cmnd 7294, HMSO, London.

BBC Licence and Agreement (1981), BBC, London.

5. J.H.Whitley to Sir Kingsley Wood (Post Master General). Letter dated 21 April, 1932. Post Office Archives, Post 33, Minute 6079, London.

6. The Times (7 July, 1936), London.

7. Report of the Broadcasting Committee, 1949 (1951), Cmnd 8116, HMSO, London.

8. Report of the Broadcasting Committee, 1960 (1962), Cmnd 1753, HMSO, London.

9. Report of the Committee on the Future of Broadcasting (1977), Cmnd 6753, HMSO, London. (Annan Committee).

10. Technic█████sory Committee, 1972 (1973), ████ers of ██████ical Sub-Committee, HMSO, ████.

11. ████ort ██████ Committee on the Future of Broadcasting (1977), ara. 14.49.

12. Report of the Committee on the Future of Broadcasting (1977), pp.215 - 217.

13. W.Whitelaw (13th November 1979) quoted in Report from the Working Party on the New Technologies, Broadcasting Research Unit, British Film Institute, London (1983), p.42.

14. W.Whitelaw (10th November 1980), House of Commons.

15. White Paper on Broadcasting (1978).

16. J.Tunstall (1983), The Media in Britain, Constable, London.

17. Advisory Council for Applied Research and Development (ACARD) (1980), Technological Change: Threats and Opportunities for the United Kingdom, HMSO, London.

18. ACARD (1980), Information Technology, HMSO, London. Forward.

19. M.Thatcher (2nd July, 1981), House of Commons.

20. J.Howkins (1982), New Technologies, New Policies? BFI, London, Ch.5.

21. Information Technology Advisory Panel (ITAP) (1982), Cable Systems, London, p.7.

22. ITAP (1982), p.53.

23. K.Baker (1982), 'Information Technology: Industrial and Employment Opportunities', The Royal Society of Arts, London, 1982, Vol.cxxx, No.5316, p.786.

24. ITAP (1982), p.48.

25. ITAP (1982), pp.7-8.

26. ITAP (1982), p.8.

27. ITAP (1982), p.8.

28. ITAP (1982), p.9.

29. Hunt Report (Inquiry into Cable Expansion and Broadcasting Policy) (1982), Cmnd 8679, HMSO, London.

30. Cable Systems and Services (1983), Cmnd 8866, HMSO, London.

31. Cable: Interim Licensing of Pilot Projects. Guidance Note. Also New Programme Services on existing cable systems. Both Home Office/Department of Trade and Industry, July 1983.

32. L.Brittan (10 June, 1982) in Report from the Working Party on the New Technologies (1983), pp. 49-50.

33. P.Fiddick (18 October 1982), The Guardian, London.

34. B.Maddox (10 June) TV: What all the rush about? The Times

35. Sir G.Jefferson (person British Telecom) (1984), The Industrial and Employment Implications of the Cable Revolution, National Economic Development Council, London.

36. The Financial Times (18 May, 1984).
37. Cable Television Association of Great Britain (1973), A Plan for Consumer Choice, London.
38. Guidance Note (1983).
39. Hunt Committee (1982).
40. Personal Interview with cable company, 1984.
41. H.Thomas (1984), in EIU Informatics, Cable and Satellite Television: Risk, Reward and Reality (1984), London, p.32.
42. Satellite and Cable TV News (May 1984), London.
43. Guidance Note (1983).
44. Report of the Working Party on the New Technologies (1983), p.291.
45. Cable and Broadcasting Bill (1984), HMSO, London.
46. Sir G.Jefferson (1984), para.61.
47. Screen Digest (April 1984), London, p.67.
48. T.Burns (1978), The BBC: Public Service and Private World, Macmillan, London.
49. BBC (1982), The Cable Debate. The BBC's reaction to the Hunt Report, BBC, London, p.34.

Chapter Five

CABLE TELEVISION IN FRANCE

Claude-Jean Bertrand

France in 1984 had practically no cable television
and, at the same time, the most ambitious and
audacious cabling programme in the world. Half the
French homes were to be cabled by the year 2000 at
a cost of 50 million F ($ 6 billion). The decisions
made by the Mitterand administration between 1982
and 1984 had started a revolution in audio-visual
communication. The goal was not merely to open new
channels for the distribution of conventional
television: it was to build an integrated network
of switched-star optical fibre cable interactive
systems carrying sound, pictures, text and data.
The project was part of the social-democratic
government's policy of modernising and decentralising
France - a Herculean task which previous governments
had never dared to tackle in a systematic way. More
specifically, the cabling programme was related to
the controlled dismantling of the Paris based state
monopoly in broadcasting and the promotion of the
electronics industry. Cable was looked upon as a
crucial element in a strategy to preserve the
prosperity of France and her culture.
    The project was a high risk gamble on the part
of a country which is usually slow in introducing
new communication technology. And the mutation in
the media initiated in the early 1980s was bound to
have deep and wide effects on French society. Yet
even the Conservative coalition which had ruled
from 1958 to 1981 expressed relatively little
opposition. If it was returned to power, it seemed
very likely that it would not fundamentally alter
the cabling policy.

HISTORICAL BACKGROUND

When radio broadcasting was started in France, it

134

was established not under the 1881 Press Act which established the freedom of the print media but under a restrictive 1837 statute on (non-electric) telecommunication and it was then entrusted as a monopoly to the PTT in 1926. Private radio stations, however, were tolerated. They made up half the total and were highly popular. But from 1945 until 1982 the monopoly was strictly enforced and the only commercial stations to serve the French public transmitted from beyond the borders (Andorra, Monaco, Saar and Luxembourg) and were at least partly controlled financially by the French state.

Television began in Paris in the 1930s but not before the 1950s did it take off and then slowly: by 1957, the French owned but 400,000 receivers. They had to wait until 1964 for a second channel, 1973 for a third and the fourth was inaugurated in 1984.

After World War 2, broadcasting did grow more autonomous administratively but it remained in the tight grip of government. The ORTF monolith set up in 1964 was broken up ten years later into 7 companies but Broadcasting Acts, in 1972 and 1974, reaffirmed the state monopoly on programming and on transmission by every means of telecommunication. The attachment to centralism was just as strong among the (Conservative) Gaullists as it was on the Left, while the 'Liberal' Giscard administration used riot police and jamming to silence the 'free' radio stations that multiplied in the 1970s.

The 1972 Act provided for some exceptions to the monopoly, for example, in closed circuit television, but it implicitly outlawed cable. Picture quality being of a high standard, the public, which paid an annual receiver's fee, did not feel the need to pay extra for any improvements. Only near the border of francophone Belgium and near the German border in partly germanophone Alsace were viewers interested in foreign programmes. Only there were a few hundred CATV systems tolerated.

In the early 1970s, however, cable seemed to be taking off in the US and Canada. Belgium was cabling fast in order to import 11 channels from its neighbours: the PTT and the public broadcasting monopoly did not object. But in France, any initiative would have to come from the state. A Société Francaise de Télédistribution (SFT) was created in 1972 by the PTT and the ORTF to build and supervise a few experimental systems. In those

years, just about all the characteristics of cable
television as conceived in the 1980s - for example,
protagonists, programming, financing - were
considered[1] but officially, as usual, the new
medium was looked upon as a mere extension of the
old.

In 1973, seven experiments were authorised to
test community television. They were to take place
in new towns or neighbourhoods: in Créteil and
Cergy-Pontoise (Paris suburbs), Rennes, Metz,
Chamonix, Grenoble and Nice. Only the Grenoble -
Echirolles project was actually carried out though
it did not last long. Four factors account for
their failure. The first factor was the lack of
public interest in schemes which did not offer
additional programmes of high quality. Local
productions in Grenoble appealed to only 10 per
cent of cabled homes. The second factor was the
economic recession . The third was the breaking up
of the ORTF which actually increased government
control on a fragmented but in no way decentralised
broadcasting system. The last factor was the
absence of government commitment Central and
local establishments feared alternative sources of
power: 'Cable distribution' wrote Le Monde 'is
still considered a "diabolical" device whose
effects should be limited by strict regulation'.[2]

In 1976, it was decreed that authorisations
for cabling would have to be granted by the Prime
Minister, that cable systems would remain state
property and that advertising would not be
permitted on cable. In the following year, in
September 1977, an executive order forbade cable
distribution of all but the three public service
channels - except in areas where foreign programmes
could be received over the air. And only TDF - the
company that had inherited the distribution
functions of the ORTF - could build and run
systems. The rationalisation was that compared to
the telephone,[3] cable was expensive and not a
priority. In its time, DBS would fare much better.

The situation in 1982
France was then a country of a little over 19 million
households, 93 per cent of which owned a television
receiver, though only 57 per cent had a colour set.
The nation was divided into 36,000 municipal units
(communes), only 500 of which contained over 30,000
inhabitants. On the other hand, a quarter of the
population lived in five urban conglomerations.
Using its microwave network, some 400

transmitters and over 7,000 low-power relays, public service television covered the whole territory. Apart from its three channels (TF 1, Antenne 2 and FR 3)[4] which all received, some French people had access to one of two commercial French language channels: Luxembourg's RTL-TV reached as far south as Reims and Monaco's RMC-TV served the Riviera. The two Belgian francophone channels were available in the north and West Germany's ARD and ZDF in Alsace. A few people watched Spain's and Italy's television along their respective, mountainous, borders.

In 1982, about 40 per cent of households were connected to a master antenna but only 3 to 4 per cent subscribed to a cable system. This ranked France 5th in the European league. About 80 urban units owned a cable system, most of which were either new towns, like Sarcelles (near Paris) or towns close to a border, like Grande Synthe (near Dunkirk). Local television, over-the-air or cable, was non-existent and so too was large scale importation and commercial networking.

THE EMERGENCE OF CABLE TELEVISION

Change was inevitable for converging national and international, political, economic and social reasons. In May 1981, Socialist Francois Mitterand was elected President and his party managed to obtain a crushing majority of seats in Parliament. For the first time in 23 years, the Left was back in power and it felt it had to innovate.

In July 1981, The Moinot Commission was appointed and its report led to the passing of the 1982 Reform Act. For the first time a law dealt explicitly with the whole of audio-visual communication, including cable (Article 1) and for the first time such communication was declared to be free (Article 2). The state gave up its monopoly of television programming. Private local radio stations were authorised on the FM band and, by 1984, over 850 were operating. Also authorised were local programming, data transfer and interactive services on cable.

De-regulation, however, was limited. Great care was taken to avoid the Italian syndrome[5] and not upset the existing balance in the media. The state retained the PTT monopoly in all telecommuni-cations, i.e. the exclusive right to establish or licence all means of audio-visual communication. A Haute Autorité de l'Audio-Visual (HA)[6] was set up to appoint the presidents of the seven public service radio and television companies, to supervise broadcasting and to award licences to local operators of radio stations and cable systems. In some cases, however, further authorisations would still have to be obtained from the government, for example, for the importation of foreign channels. In spite of its 110 Articles, the 1982 Act was a skeleton loi cadre which remained to be fleshed out by implementation decrees. It was only two years later, and after many compromises, that a Cable Act was passed and this contained many of the necessary details and specifications.

The new deal in audio-visual communication fitted in with the government's policy of political decentralisation, aiming at more democracy and more economic and social efficiency. But many other factors were involved. The first was public dissatisfaction with the status quo. This was emphasised by the success of the 'pirate' radio stations, by the increased attendance at cinemas and by the sudden rush on VCRs in the early 1980s. A 1983 poll indicated that 73 per cent of French viewers urgently wanted more diversified programming.[7] Both mismanagement and union abuse had survived the ORTF: the broadcasting units stood accused of huge bureaucratic waste, both of money and creativity, which competition within the monopoly had only worsened. Public radio and television were criticised for providing too much elitist culture and too few entertainment programmes - not to speak of government controlled news. The dissatisfaction was intensified in the early 1980s by hostile campaigns led by the (mostly Conservative) press and by public awareness of alternatives.

The second factor was industrial. Cable was finally booming in North America. West Germany and Britain were about to cable their respective countries and the French electronics industry which ranked only third in Europe - and very far behind the world leaders, Japan and the US - argued that France could not afford to repeat its past failures (e.g. with computers or more recently with VCRs). There was not just an economic need to prolong the huge effort made to spread the telephone, but 'the great French electronics boom of the mid 1970s and onwards'[8] also had to be sustained. From July 1982 onwards, the Mitterand administration decided to systematically promote the filière électronique, that is, all high technology industries and services considered as an integrated whole. It was

to have priority in the ninth Five Year Plan
(1984-1988). Over five years, 140 billion Francs ($
16 billion) were to be spent. Hence the filière was
a major part of the programme to restructure the
French economy for the post-industrial era and,
among other goals, to create jobs.

This effort was clearly aimed at international
markets, but it was also directed at the domestic
one. In the electronics sector, France in 1982 had
imported 13.5 billion F more than it had exported.
Moreover, data transmission among business firms
was increasing by 30 per cent a year and the PTT
believed that French households would soon require
a second telephone line for videotex and other
services.

Last, but by no means least, was a concern to
develop a programme production industry for both
economic and cultural purposes. The monopoly of
public broadcasting of the airwaves had so stifled
creativity, especially in the field of mass
culture, that many feared that France was incapable
not only of competing on the international scene
but of resisting a foreign (meaning American)
cultural invasion.

THE CABLE PLAN

In June 1984, the French Parliament passed the
Cable Television Bill. This, in effect, confirmed
the Plan Câble which had been adopted by the
Cabinet in November 1982 under great pressure from
the PTT. The Plan stressed that over a period of
15 years it would be necessary to cable about 15
million households. This decision threw a long
shadow over proposals for DBS, even though it was
understood that cable television and DBS were
complementary. The previous administration had, in
1979, inaugurated a project to launch a DBS
service, TDF 1, in 1983; by mid 1984, the launch of
TDF 1 - by then thought to be much too expensive
and technologically out of date - had been
postponed to late 1986.

The ultimate goal in cabling was not merely to
develop means of supplying viewers with more
television entertainment since that would not
justify the investment. It was to build a réseau
numérique à l'intégration de services (RNIS). an
Integrated Service Digital Network (ISDN), a
broadband cable network integrating all electonic
technologies, new (from satellites to home
computers) and old (from the telephone to recorded

music), so as to serve the communication requirements of business, of government and of private citizens. Although the general approach was untypically flexible and pragmatic, some basic choices were firmly made which blended tradition and innovation and were thus to mark out the French cable project as quite original.

The boldest decision was to use fibre optics and the switched-star configuration. Starting from scratch made it possible to impose a standard. What made it necessary were the two ultimate objects of the plan: to blend television and telephone within a single interactive network and to develop an avant garde technology for export. Further advantages were easier installation, signal quality, security since no scrambling was necessary, addressability, easy audience measurement and unlimited extensibility.

A second bold decision was financial. The state alone would supply the enormous investments needed to cable the country although it would share control with system operators and programme providers who would draw their income from fees, subscriptions for special services, pay-per-view and advertising.

A third decision was, in a French context, stunning. The state would supervise the planning and building of systems it paid for and it would have a hand in their operation but the initiative for cabling a community would have to come from the local government and the cable operator would be a société locale d'exploitation du câble (SLEC), normally a joint venture of local government and private interests, a société d'économie mixte (as defined in a law dated 7th July 1983). In practice, a town council could farm out the building and running of its system to a business firm. A system could draw up to 80 per cent of its income from advertising. Programme providers, apart from the public service broadcasting organisations, would also be largely private. For France, this blend of state, municipal and private control, balancing desire for fast expansion and a concern for the public interest represented radical de-regulation.

Cable Programmes and Services
These would be of two kinds. One kind would be immediately available and this would include the attractive radio and television programmes which were so much in demand. The other kind would be gradually phased in: in the long term such

interactive services would be more profitable. Both kinds of fare would either be locally originated or imported from within, or from without, the country, via conventional networks or satellites.

As regards the first category, some rules were set out in 1984:

- systems must carry the public broadcasting channels;
- foreign channels (including Luxembourg's RTL-TV And Monaco's RMC-TV) must not take up more than 30 per cent of a system's capacity;
- 60 per cent of the films shown must come from the EEC and 50 per cent from francophone countries;
- films could only be shown 3 years after their release as on the public broadcasting networks;
- 15 per cent of a system's capacity must be devoted to 'local programming';
- the same restrictions applied to advertising on cable as on the public broadcasting networks.

As the global audience grew and the number of activated channels increased from about 9 to a planned 30, basic and premium television entertainment channels are expected to be supplemented by others dedicated, for instance, to news or to education (a field almost totally neglected by the broadcast networks), or to serving special audiences such as immigrant groups.

As for interactive services, the opportunities were limitless and it was forecast that they would eventually constitute the major offering.[9] France was quite advanced in what she called télématique, that is, telecommunications and computing[10] and especially in teletext (Antiope) and videotex (Minitel) for mass public services including the telephone directory. Those developments had been promoted before 1981 in the Plan Télématique. Data banks were being organised by, for example, travel agencies, publishers and mail order firms, and in such areas as sound, video and games programmes. Opinion surveys showed public interest in all new services, particularly as microcomputers multiplied in offices and homes along with videogame units and VCRs. Such services as burglar, fire and health alarms, meter-reading, temperature controls or electronic mail go naturally with interactivity as,

141

of course, does the telephone and even the videophone.

THE ACTORS IN CABLE

The success of the Plan Câble depended on the co-operation of many different, sometimes antagonistic, public and private bodies. That, and the high stakes involved, accounted for the 18 month delay between the announcement of the Plan and its enactment.

Central state institutions

Many agencies were implicated, such as the Ministries of the Interior, of Industry, of Education, of Culture, of Youth and Sports and of Communication. But, in addition, five other bodies were assigned major duties within the overall undertaking.

The first was the Mission TV Câble (also known as the Mission Schreiner) which included representatives of all the ministries concerned. It was set up in December 1982 to help local authorities develop cable projects and to co-ordinate their efforts. It was to define the main objectives, to examine applications for cabling and to provide towns with research funds and expert advice, to work at making the existing programmes available to SLECs and to expand production. Its approach was strictly pragmatic.

The second public body was the non-governmental Haute Autorité (HA). It would be in charge of granting licences to SLECs after approving their programme plans. In 1984, the HA participated in the determination of general policy but wished to delay regulating until cable had started operating in earnest.

The PTT, and more particularly its Direction Générale des Télécommunications (DGT), has been active in cable for many years. It wants to establish a fibre optic cable network for telecommunication[11] irrespective of whether that network is also used for entertainment purposes. Its main tasks, in this respect, are to authorise all building work and either to supervise it or to participate directly in it. These tasks would ensure that the network was compatible and allowed for interconnections. The PTT would also finance the whole operation and so remain the sole owner as well as the organisation in charge of maintenance. It is worth noting that 'today's PTT is the most

modern nationwide sales, marketing, services and
maintenance organisation in the country'.[12]
    Another body very much concerned with cable is
TDF. Since 1980 it has lain under the twin
authorities of the Ministries of Communication and
of the PTT so that its activities could be
harmonised with those of the other communication
carrier, the DGT. In the cable field, TDF was to
focus its interest on the head-end, that is, on the
conception, erection, hardware, and maintenance as
well as personnel training. This would normally
include a satellite and microwave receiving
station, a 'centre de programmation' and a 'régie
d'exploitation'. The DGT could own it fully, partly
or not at all just as it could, or not, take part in
the management of the system.
    The last of the state agencies to play a
crucial role in cable is the Caisse des dépôts et
consignations (CDC), a reserve bank with which
non-profit, state insured savings institutions such
as the national health system, are required to
deposit their funds. Since the 1950s, a function of
the CDC has been to provide loans and expert advice
to local communities for their development
projects. In the early 1980s, it was planning to
enter the communications sector and it too jumped
on the cable bandwagon. In late 1983, it made 1.5
billion F ($170 million) available to urban units
wishing to lay cable.[13]

Corporate Partners.
Two big corporations which, like the CDC, had long
experience of dealing with town councils also
seemed interested in expanding into cable. One
signed an agreement with the PTT for promoting
cable as early as March 1983. But both the
Compagnie Générale des Eaux and the Compagnie
Lyonnaise des Eaux - utility companies that run
water distribution systems in thousands of towns
and villages - were private concerns.
    In contrast to broadcasting, cable has been
opened wide to business enterprises. Both industrial
firms and programme producers were expected to
invest 1.5 to 2 billion F ($170 to $200 million)
each by the mid 1980s. The French electric and
electricity industry had annual sales of 180
billion F ($20 billion) whereas cable proper would
only represent 40 billion F ($4.5 billion) over 10
years. But cable was to offer a remarkable
showcase. Firms organised for it. For instance, the
Groupement des industries électroniques (GIEL) had

set up a special commission on cable to promote collaboration between firms and negotiations with the government. Subsidiaries of two giants, Thomson-CSF and St. Gobain, had formed a special company to go into cable and there were other examples.

While industrialists accepted PTT supervision, they opposed its participation. They wished to be associated in the management systems in order to acquire the experience and capacity to deliver turn-key cable systems overseas. However, it should be remembered that the four largest firms in the filière électronique had been nationalised by the Mitterand administration: Thomson, CII-Honeywell Bull, Compagnie Generale d'Electricite (CGE) and Matra. These four, between them, account for half the production and more than half the exports in this sector. The process of nationalisation had enabled the government to rationalise the industry. All telecommunications activities of Thomson and CGE went to CIT-Alcatel, a subsidiary of CGE which then became the central firm in the French cable project. Before 1981, the optical fibre industry had been restructured around two pole-firms: Fibres optiques industries (FOI), controlled by St. Gobain and Thomason-CSF, and Compagnie Lyonnaise de transmissions optique (CLTO), owned by a division of CGE.

Programme Providers

Programming was from the outset a major concern. Which institutions owned, or could produce, material suitable for cable? The best reserve of programmes was held by the Institut National de l'Audiovisuel (INA): it stores all the products of public broadcasting after they have been commercially exploited for five years and it possesses a computerised general catalogue (IMAGO). The INA enabled the Mission Schreiner to gather 2,000 hours of programming by the spring of 1984.

In 1984, the three television networks and public radio's three networks had all shown interest in producing for cable whereas a decade earlier the ORTF had stonewalled all new media.[14] Both Antenne 2 and TF 1 had set up a multi-purpose subsidiary to co-operate with cable. FR 3, which in 1983 had started to regionalise production in earnest, was actively supporting 3 of the 12 pilot local cable projects (see below). The fourth (pay-television) network, Canal Plus, might, in the future, find it advantageous to sell its programming at a discount to cable systems.

Radio France's three networks and multiplying regional stations could provide a great deal of audio material for cable,[15] as could hundreds of private stations whose estimated listening audience is about 5 million. Cable could also make it possible to satisfy applicants for radio licences that were kept off the air for lack of frequencies. As regards the three 'peripheral' commercial stations, both RTL and RMC wish to expand their television activities. In 1984, RTL was video-taping its most popular radio programmes for possible use on cable and Europe 1 was getting ready to supply 5 hours per day to cable systems even though it had no television channel.

A major supplier would be the cinema. Not only did the Archives du film contain 70,000 films and the Cinémathèque 30,000, but the French industry has remained exceptionally healthy. In 1981, 180 and in 1982, 164 feature films were made and these figures exclude co-productions and pornographic material. In fact, Gaumont, a major film distributer, has suggested a film channel for cable.

Accordingly to Article 81 of the 1982 Act, there were to be no American style commercial cable programming networks but for economic reasons, régies de programmes, or networks, were approved by the Haute Autorité and encouraged by the Mission Schreiner in the belief that the market could support between 20 to 25 such networks. Organisations interested in such networks include the wire-services (AFP and ACP), the print media (for example, the daily Libération), book publishers, music publishers and distributors of video cassettes.

Finally, foreign suppliers and such regular programme broadcasters as the BBC or satellite networks such as the Sky Channel have also shown an interest in supplying cable systems. These services are, in fact, immediately available and may satisfy the demand for imported material which surveys have continually documented.[16]

THE LOCAL CABLE SYSTEM

The official target is to cable all (or most) urban households before the year 2000. But, in fact, much will depend on local governments. Many are likely to show an interest as most other major investment programmes such as sewage, electricity and telephones have already been completed.

Legally, a cable system could not be larger

than 60 km in any one of its dimensions or cover more than two of the 95 départements. Economically, cable was not considered viable in a town of less than 100,000 inhabitants or with less than about 20,000 subscribers.

The intention was that a town, or group of suburban towns, would first apply to the PTT and at the same time contact the Mission Schreiner. Feasibility studies would then be carried out to determine local needs and the availability of local partners and to draw up a policy to ensure economic viability. If the ensuing project was deemed acceptable, the area would be added to the DGT waiting list. In theory, a municipality could opt to build at its own expenses; indeed, it would be compelled to do so if it insisted on using co-axial cable for a tree and branch system because it found it less expensive and quite sufficient for what the average person wanted, that is, more television entertainment. In practice, however, this option was non-existent.

As noted above, the cable system would be run by a SLEC. The SLEC had to be a societe d'economie mixte, a joint public/private venture familiar to city councils. But, this time, there would be a major difference: while the chairman had to be an elected official, the local government was <u>not</u> required to be the majority stockholder though it had to retain a blocking minority share. Also, one seat had to go to a representative of the state. As of mid 1984, no entity, except the state, was entitled to hold stock in more than one SLEC (Article 80). This ruling was meant to prevent huge American style MSOs. It was, however, possible to amend this rule and the Mission TV Cable could recommend a limit of 5 majority holdings and no limit for minority holdings. A municipality could thus opt for one of the following:

- it could run the whole enterprise on its own;
- it could let a private agency run the enterprise;
- it could devise a plan for balanced public/private co-operation.

The SLEC is to be in charge of all decisions regarding programming and contracts with suppliers; it would determine the commercial policy of the system and collect the subscription fees and it would also have to pay the PTT for use of the lines

Cable Television in France

and the TDF for the head-end. All this was in accordance with its cahiers des charges- its legal and self-imposed obligations - as approved by the Haute Autorité.

Municipalities were also to part fund the construction of the cable systems. In 1984, it was officially estimated that the average cost per home cabled was in the region of 4,500 F (about $500). The actual cost was much higher, between 11 and 15 thousand Francs ($1300 and $1700). Originally, municipalities were to pay 30 per cent of the cost for half the households passed; this was considered the 'normal' penetration rate with 40 per cent being the minimum penetration rate. This contribution was an advance which would be reimbursed to the municipalities by the PTT. The idea was to involve the local authorities financially and the rationale was that they would, as it were, pay the cost for the installation of a co-axial system while the state paid the extra cost of installing a fibre optic system. In June 1984, however, the PTT-SLEC contract was made negotiable, with the provision that the more the municipality paid the faster it would be cabled up.

Commercial viability could, it was said, be attained with 15 to 20 thousand homes cabled and systems could start operating with about 3,000 subscribers. A SLEC was expected to break even within about 5 years. Its expenses would be equally divided between programming, operating costs and rental fees. Its revenues would come from installation fees, subscriptions to basic programme services, subscriptions to pay-television channels and payments by programmers out of their advertising or sponsorship revenue. In practice, three very different commercial policies could be implemented and found to be generally acceptable:

- universal cabling with the initial stress on interactive services. The cost would then be included in the local rates as is planned in Genevilliers (near Paris);
- a low penetration policy - at the 25 per cent level - with high costs charged to subscribers and no use made of the municipal budget. This policy is being considered for Paris;
- a combination of the above with a 50 per cent penetration rate as projected in Montpellier.

147

Irrespective of the policy adopted, the subscriber would still have to meet certain expenses. It is estimated that the initial house connection would be in the region of 800 F ($100), that the basic cable service will cost between 600 F and 800 F (about $100)and that the subscriber would have to pay anything up to 1,800 F ($220) for extra products and services.

As regards programming, the 9 original channels were expected to fall into three categories: must carry, advertising financed or sponsored services and premium services. At the beginning, the Mission Schreiner would provide a computerised catalogue accessible by Minitel (videotex) terminal. But SLECs would probably dedicate whole channels to régies de programme, or cable-feeding networks.

What of local programmes? The legal minimum of 15 per cent which cable systems were to carry included both programmes whose rights the SLEC had itself acquired and local products proper. The latter category was likely to remain at the 5 to 10 per cent level. The emphasis was on the necessity of local programming rather than any of the idealism of the early 1970s concerning community television. Surveys confirmed a demand for such local material so long as it dealt with everyday life and also provided useful services.

THE DEVELOPMENT OF CABLE IN 1984

In May 1984, the PTT Minister announced that 133 urban areas had officially applied to be cabled. This included all the towns with more than 100,000 inhabitants. Altogether, this represented about 4 million households. The Minister also confirmed that equipment for 320,000 homes had been ordered from LTT-Thomson and Velec-CGCT for 1984. One third would be in co-axial cable (0 generation) and the rest in optical fibre (1st generation). This represented a positive, if small, start to cable's development in France.

The Twelve Pilot Projects

In 1984, the Mission TV Cable granted priority status to 12 towns. All of these owned either old cable systems which needed to be upgraded and extended or new, state-of-the-art, experimental ones.

The most special case was certainly Biarritz, a seaside resort in south west France. It had the largest, most sophisticated, cable experiment in the world and an experiment which was not meant to be applied universally since the cost per home cabled was in the region of 400,000 F ($46,000). In September 1984, 34 out of a planned 1,500 homes and offices were linked by a switched-star fibre system which could be extended to 30,000 subscribers sometime in the future. By mid 1985 subscribers will have access to 15 video channels, 12 radio channels, videotex, interactive data bank access and the videophone. The object of the Biarritz experiment was to test the concept, the equipment, the installation and the management and maintenance of a large scale exercise and to assess the needs and interests of private and business users. It was also an important international showcase.

As it owned no cable system, Montpellier was not included in the 1983 list of pilot projects though it seems proper to include it here. It had plans to build a city-wide fully optical system, the first in the world after Biarritz, in 1986 in a new neighbourhood, Antigone, as part of its desire to become a hi-technology metropolis. The system will connect 50,000 homes by 1990.

Lille, a northern industrial city with 1.6 million inhabitants, also has experimental status. Its 50 homes cable system began in January 1984 and it aims to test both the technology and the potential audience. The second stage of this experiment is to involve 3,000 homes by 1986 and the third stage will take in 300,000 homes by 1990. During the first phase, Lille planned to offer 15 television channels which would include 4 Belgian, 2 Dutch, 3 British and 1 Swiss channel in addition to RTL and RMC. Eventually, there would be 30 video channels and 20 audio ones.

Metz is an eastern city with 120,000 inhabitants close to the German border. In 1978, it was granted an exemption from the 1977 broadcasting regulations with the effect that the TDF was able to award a 30 year cable franchise to CENOD, a Philips subsidiary. The result is that, in 1984, Metz is the only major city which has a large scale co-axial cable system. The 5,200 homes that subscribe to the system have access to 9 television channels which include 2 Belgian, 3 German services and RTL-TV and 12 audio channels. In the future another 31,000 can be connected and 20 more video channels activated. The main reason for the rather low penetration rate of 22 per cent is that most potential subscribers already possess multi-standard sets and antennas and are, therefore, unwilling to pay more - even only 50 F per month more ($6) - for mere CATV services.

Also close to a border and classified as a 'new town' is Grande Synthe, near Dunkirk. Its co-axial cable system was started in 1975 by the town council. Thanks to the local taxes paid by one of the largest French steel mills, it could simply decide the rate of penetration: 8,200 homes for 26,000 inhabitants. Out of its potential 15 channels, it operated only 9 in 1984 and one of these was a local channel.

The town which came top of the Mission's list was the new town of Cergy-Pontoise, a suburb of Paris with 120,000 inhabitants. It has had a co-axial cable system since its construction in 1971 and its system is now the largest in France. The towns population has shown a great deal of interest in cable television, particularly during two specific cable experiments. By the end of 1984, the system will carry the 3 must carry channels, Canal Plus, TV 5[17], Sky Chanel, 2 other francophone channels and a further local one. By then, half of its 20,000 CATV homes will be linked up to the head-end. Three other towns have similar characteristics: Marne le Vallée, Evry (near Paris) and I'Isle d'Abeau (near Lyon).

Somewhat different is the case of Rennes[18] in Brittany which was the first town to sign an agreement with the Mission in February 1984. Three of its suburbs have been cabled since 1973 but the system is not in operation. The agreement makes it possible to connect 4,500 homes by the end of 1984. Some of these homes will be equipped with fibre optic lines though the rest of the town will eventually be linked up by optical fibres.

The other areas on the Mission's list of 12 were the La Villeneuve district of Grenoble, Nancy and Sarcelles, a new town north of Paris.

Other towns with plans for cable developments
The most important of these is Paris since nothing is quite accepted in France without Parisian consecration. The city council has entered into a 51/49 per cent partnership with the Société Lyonnaise des Eaux, the water utility. In the future, it is possible that some press concerns will also join this partnership. By the beginning of 1985, 46,000 homes in the 13th and 15th arrondissements - districts already equipped with co-axial cable for master antenna services - will be connected by optical fibre to a central head-

Cable Television in France

end. By 1986, 55,000 more homes should be cabled
and by 1990 between one half and 1 million homes.
The mayor of Paris and opposition leader, J.
Chirac, is determined to obtain a large degree of
programming freedom so as to ensure the profitability
of the system and so avoid increases in local
taxation. The system hopes to carry 9 channels,
including RTL-TV, RMC-TV, Canal Plus, a British
channel and two 'local' channels (one Parisian, the
other a film and sports channel).

One other area deserves to be cited. Vaux le
Pénil, a town of Seine-et-Marne (east of Paris) had
formed a partnership with Canadian MSO Videotron to
finance, build and manage a co-axial cable system.
This plan had the co-operation of numerous
neighbouring communities. The plan projected a 50
per cent penetration rate in an area of 300,000
homes and it was hoped to start constructing the
system in the autumn of 1984. Ten, of the eventual
30 channels, were to be devoted to conventional
television, two others to local programming and the
rest to services such as tele-shopping. The whole
project, however, soon collapsed; a major cause of
the collapse was the fierce opposition of the PTT.
It would only permit exceptions to its all fibre
optic objectives in areas where cable systems
existed prior to 1982 as in Grande Synthe, Metz or
Nice.

At the end of 1984, it appeared as if the
pilot projects were stagnating and fading away
whilst some non-pilot projects were being developed
rapidly in places such as Boulogne/St.Cloud/Sèvres/
Suresnes, a group of suburbs west of Paris.

PROBLEMS

By the middle of 1984, the statutory framework for
cable development had been set out and actual
cabling was in progress but many problems had yet
to be resolved.

Political Problems
Any new medium of social communication is bound to
have an impact on politics. What of a 'super-medium'
such as cable in a country as centralised as
France? No one really knew what its impact would be
and many were extremely apprehensive. Some of the
problems which cropped up were of a narrow, party
political, kind. Not only were there conflicts
between the DGT and TDF technocracies but there
were also problems of conflict between all the

151

ministries concerned. Each kept defending its own constituency[19] and/or tried to get a larger share of the cable cake. Just as narrowly political was the concern of the party in power to survive the 1986 legislative and the 1988 presidential elections. From 1983 onwards, a growing majority of the public has turned hostile to the left. Rapid decentralisation and privatisation could provide weapons to the right wing opposition.

More generally, such was the change initiated and the risks taken, that all ideological, political and bureaucratic forces felt concerned over three fundamental issues:

- central versus local control;
- public service versus commercial audio-visual communication;
- entertainment communication as against interactive services.

Positions did not neatly correspond to the Right/Left division. Both sides bandied about words like freedom, democracy, culture and economic development. There were some who disapproved of all the basic options. These were the advocates of either the status quo or of privatised over-the-air broadcasting or DBS. Almost everyone else was somewhat displeased by the governmental compromises between controlled expansion and de-regulation. Some vacillation on the part of the government and the vagueness of many decisions gave them cause for fear and for further militancy.

At the local level, the problems were numerous. Local authorities might not only find it hard to handle political decentralisation and cable at one and the same time but they were not at all used to dealing with matters of audio-visual communication. Local establishments had always judged it more convenient to let central government take charge. They looked upon unscreened, group-to-group, popular communication as subversive. The pressure for legislation of CB radio and local radio stations, for example, had certainly not come from them.

Among the local opposition, there was also a fear that cable systems could become political instruments in the hands of the town council majority as was the case with municipal magazines. What criteria would SLECs use to allocate channels? Would minority groups have access? Might not all channels be farmed out to agents of big, even multinational, corporations? Political independence would then even be more difficult to preserve at local than at national level.[20]

Legal Problems

Legal scholars had paid little attention to other media than the printed press. And what little literature there was concerned broadcasting.[21] Yet cable involved so many contradictory interests that strife was bound to abound especially in the early absence of precise regulations. What, for instance, should be done about advertising on imported EEC channels which violated French laws?

Probably the most serious problem was copyright and then not only for foreign programmes. For the inaugural year, 1984, the Mission Schreiner negotiated the payment of a symbolic Franc to the copyright agencies. If only to encourage programme production, fair and simple solutions would have to be devised.

Social Problems

The two major concerns here were those of fairness and responsiveness. One of the Mission's assignments was to sound out the public. Surveys in 1983 showed that 3 out of every 5 French people had heard of cable but other findings were vague and contradictory. The problem was that the French had had no experience of cable - no more than Americans had of television in 1939 when a CBS-NBC survey indicated that 83 per cent of them did not wish to have the new medium.[22]

When systems did start operating, should the subscriber be treated as a consumer or as a citizen? Should the public be given what they like, that is, entertainment, or what they need, that is, education and information? This was an old controversy, especially between Marxists and entrepreneurs but to the extent that this dilemma truly exists, channel rich cable might not be able to solve it.

The other preoccupation was to guarantee that everybody would be served equally. Some areas would be more expensive to cable than others: their inhabitants should not have to pay more. Rural zones would not be cabled early on, if ever: would LPTV stations, terrestrial satellites and DBS compensate? Basic cable, not to speak of pay cable, would cost subscribers at least three times more than the annual television licence fee which would still have to be paid. Would not the new medium be out of reach of all the lower income population?

Technical and Industrial Problems

The cabling of France, was in itself, an enormous task but it was rendered all the more staggering by the choice of fibre optics for the system. When, in 1969, it was decided to end the scarcity of telephones in France, a vast industrial effort was needed but at least the technology was a familiar one. This is not the case with fibre optics. It is not only unfamiliar but it is not even fully developed. Whereas trunk lines no longer offer any difficulty, the equipment at both ends does: switching video signals is still an immense problem. A whole range of expensive electronic and other hardware has to be used to convert signals from optical ones to electronic ones and back again.

French industry knew how to produce optical fibres, although it had only really started to do so in 1980-81. The problem was the production capacity especially as switched-star networks require much larger quantities of cable than tree and branch ones. Whereas cabling 1 million homes a year would consume 300,000 kilometres, the 1984 French annual capacity was only 30,000 kilometres. And that capacity was growing rather slowly as manufacturers remained bearish about domestic and export markets. Only orders for cabling 500,000 homes a year could trigger off investment and then mass production would take several years. The danger was that many towns would remain on the PTT waiting list for years and would then be tempted to franchise private companies to build co-axial cable systems for video distribution which might turn out to be incompatible with the future national grid.

Financial Problems

No one could accurately estimate the final cost of the whole project. Even short term predictions were unreliable: it was a shock in 1983 to discover that with optical fibre the cost per household cabled would be three times the amount forecast by the PTT.

The two fundamental problems were that profitability would eventually come from video communication but that cable development had to be paid for initially by mass tele-distribution and that the number of subscribers to, and advertisers on, cable would at best grow only as fast as systems and programmes multiplied. Indeed, VCRs, the pay-TV channel, Canal Plus, and DBS might siphon off much of the potential audience during the first crucial years when the market was small and big investments yet to be made. What made matters worse were two government requirements: firstly, that cable be developed fast and not be restricted to wealthy groups in society and, secondly, that cable be put on a sound financial basis and yet not jeopardise long term economic balances.

Not only were manufacturers and programme producers hesitant about taking the plunge but so too were local governments. They would have to finance preliminary studies, undertake to construct a fibre optic system they did not feel they needed - and which they would not own - and then only provide a minimum of local origination. The CDC intended to include its cabling loans within the general credit package available to a town and so a town might have to choose between, say, a cable system and a new swimming pool. In any event, systems could not break even for 4 to 9 years depending on penetration. These official estimates were based on a penetration rate of 15 per cent in the first year and 50 per cent within 5 years but at half the anticipated subscription rate Metz only had 22 per cent penetration after 5 years. Another consideration was that cable might kill off the local cinemas and also hurt other leisure interests. It appeared as if cable communications would first serve big firms, then smaller businesses and only then would it serve the local citizens. Moreover, the PTT planned to keep all the profits.

Cultural Problems
These have attracted more attention than technical and commercial issues. Because of its former cultural hegemony, France harbours an obsession with cultural imperialism. In the early 1980s Americanisation seemed to increase, while the recent Italian debacle stood as a dreaded warning of what could happen. So, besides the contempt of the intellectuals for contemporary popular entertainment - most of it made in the USA - pride in French culture and fear of alienation generated great concern for programming. In fact, that was the theme of the only book to have been entirely devoted to French cable, _Images pour le câble_.[23]

Cable's multiple channels would be voracious

gobblers of programmes. The stocks of the ORTF - largely unappealing black and white material - and of TF 1, Antenne 2 and FR 3 would soon be used up and they would, in any case, be re-runs. One reserve of (never) broadcast material was the video material produced by scattered individuals or groups over the years, but these needed to be located, duplicated and listed in computerised catalogues. As regards new productions, with cable audiences small for many years to come, commercial motivation would be low and state subsidies probably necessary even if the needed facilities and technical and creative manpower were available which they were not on either a local or regional level. This paucity of production has been the result of 30 years of centralised state monopoly and, within it, of the oligopoly enjoyed by a handful of producers.

Whole channels could be imported live from abroad but the non-francophone ones would require captions and much of the programming would have little appeal for most French audiences. The other solution would be to buy selected foreign programmes and films and then dub them. But most of the material is not only commercial mass entertainment fare but also of American origin. Indeed, while European nations found it hard to co-operate, US suppliers were ready to pounce: HBO, the largest American programmer for cable, had tried to buy a share of Canal Plus; the satellite transponded Sky Channel was already pouring American entertainment into European cable systems; Luxembourg seemed ready to endorse the American Coronet which looked much more like a cable serving satellite than a DBS service. The decline of the francophone Belgian RTBF television channels as a result of foreign competition carried by cable systems seemed a sign of things to come.

The problem was not just to expand the cultural industries[24] in order to supply the domestic media but their productions could slow down the erosion of French cultural positions abroad. If, at last, they geared themselves up for export, they could take advantage of the spread of programme hungry new media and possibly enter hitherto closed territories, like the USA. As President Mitterand had stressed, 'cultural industries are the industries of the future;.... investing in culture means investing in the economy'.

Cable Television in France

Media Problems
One reason for the freeze on media development during the 1960s and 1970s had been the concern not to upset the existing media equilibrium. In the early 1980s, that concern still existed. While cable would offer an opportunity to other media, it would still be a threat to them, both in its tele-distribution and its video-communication phases.

The most obvious danger was to the three broadcasting networks. First, their revenues could not be maintained or increased if their audiences declined dramatically. And cable would also compete for their revenues from advertising. Secondly, the strict and rigid obligations set out in their respective charters rendered them uncompetitive. In the early part of 1984, all three network presidents publicly expressed rebellion. The Minister of Communication told them that they were free to enter all the media fields and had five years to prove their mettle yet no shackles were removed.

A year before its launch, the president of Canal Plus declared: 'Cable, there's the enemy!'.He hoped to gain an audience before large cities were cabled but who would pay 120 Francs a month ($14) for Canal Plus' single movie channel when on cable they could, for the same price, get 9 channels, including a film channel, as was the case in Paris?

As regards radio, while the 'peripheral' commercial stations had no fear of cable, the local stations were worried about audio-visual competition for what little local advertising was not monopolised by the daily and weekly press. It should be remembered that French advertising expenditures, in proportion to Gross National Product, were among the lowest in Northern Europe, 0.53 per cent compared with 0.83 per cent in West Germany and 1.35 per cent in Great Britain. This was partly due to an absence of real competition between media as the huge increase of advertising in Italy had recently proved.

The cinema in France had remained more productive than in other comparable nations and kept more of its audience coming to its network of theatres, the most modern in the world. It was also the second largest exporter of films after Hollywood. Thus it had better resisted American penetration. But would not cable cripple it just as commercial television had choked the Italian cinema unless it was strictly regulated?

The major problem was that facing the news-

157

paper press which, in France, is overwhelmingly regional. Cable, and especially its use for videotex, threatened both sales and advertising revenues. The press had had to cope with its own technological revolution - from offset to VDTs - while its share of the national advertising budget had declined from 77 per cent in 1968 to 58.5 per cent in 1982. Its first reaction was either to ignore cable or to fight it - this had been its reaction to local radio. In 1984, it clearly wanted to join in in cable enterprises but, besides its reluctance to enter a state regulated institution, it remained, as ever, legally excluded from the audio-visual field. That seemed 'professionally absurd, technologically archaic and economically dangerous'.[25] In the days of multi-media enterprises, how could the press be kept out of a medium such as cable. On the other hand, in the absence of a strong national press, the regional or local monopoly of French newspapers was a regrettable enough phenomenon not to be expanded.

CONCLUSION

Cabling France is 'a venture essential for our country, our culture, our heritage, our capacity for creation, our national identity', declared the Minister of Communication at the first national cable conference in Marne la Vallée in 1983. In contrast, the Minister of PTT warned that 'even if we progress with determination, cable television is not for tomorrow'.[26] The Plan Câble was too ambitious not to engender both enthusiasm and fierce criticism. Which would it be: another Ariane or another Concorde?

Some of the negative judgements could be discounted: they belonged to political knee-jerk rhetoric. As the daily Libération in reference to the former Premier and opposition leader Chirac, put it 'he and his friends proved incapable to innovate and now they go tooth and nail for a government which has begun achieving what they could not do'.[27] Parallel to the politically motivated detractor went that French type, the neurotic patriot who believes that whatever other nations do, or don't do, is better: the French approach to cable being different from that of the Japanese, Americans and Germans could therefore only be wrong.

Much of the criticism was sound, however. For champions of free enterprise, the Plan reeked of

Cable Television in France

old-fashioned state dirigisme, even of socialism. Not only did the 1982 and 1984 Acts establish state supervision over cable but also state participation in its construction and management. Worse, they gave the state indirect control over programming, thus negating the government's claim of having introduced openness and pluralism into social communication. Opinions voiced within the majority Socialist Party - not to speak of the Communists - could generate misgivings as could several doctrinaire decisions, like the early ban on advertising for private local radio stations or, outside the communications fields, the 1982 nationalisations and the 1983 re-kindling of the public versus regligious 'school war'. According to free-enterprisers, nothing would do short of Reagan style total de-regulation.[28] They would, as businessmen, profit from cable financially, and, as conservatives, they could thus regain the political control over radio and television which they had enjoyed from 1958 to 1981 and whose loss they had never ceased grieving over.

Cynics saw the Plan Câble as a new outbreak of that old French malady: devising glorious projects, debating them for years, making utopian decisions and finally realising nothing, if only because money is unavailable. Close to the cynics stood some realists. For them, the state of the economy was so poor that France could not afford such expense, at least in the short run, especially with fibre optic technology being so new. Low public demand, lack of commercial incentives and official red tape would also be unsurpassable obstacles. Most local projects would probably be quietly snuffed out by the PTT, except for a few showcases like Biarritz and Paris. Popular craving for diversity would be satisfied with more over-the-air local and/or commercial television, probably using DBS services.

Other realists were not so much pessimistic as circumspect. They found too much about the Plan Câble remained unclear, for example, the division of responsibility between the government and the Haute Autorité. Besides, considering the variable flexibility of the government, it was impossible to tell whether changes would be made that might contribute to the viability of the enterprise, say, in allowing other bodies than the state to own shares in more than one SLEC.

One last group of critics consisted of humanists and left-wingers. Both feared the

159

corrupting power of money and wanted audio-visual communication to remain public services. Their model was the BBC and their bugbear was American commercial broadcasting. Moreover, they were quite certain that the de-monopolisation brought about by cable would open borders to a cultural invasion by Hollywood and Wall Street combined.

Needless to say, in 1984 the optimists were also legion. They considered that, at long last, an essential break had been made with the past which allowed France to enter the post-industrial age. The impetus could not now be stalled: the nation would be cabled before the year 2000. All problems could be solved by compromises between the protagonists since, after all, 'most of the levers of power are held by the well-known French meritocracy whose main actors, whether in public or private industry, or governments, are all largely part of the same network based on the same Grandes Écoles'.[29]

Politically, 'what is most striking is the consensus on general lines. Majority and opposition are agreed on basics', wrote Y.Agnes in Le Monde.[30] The Socialists understand the need for partial privatisation and for competition, while the Gaullists could not jettison their Jacobin attachment to the state irrespective of what they had said publicly after the state had gone Socialist. Both had accepted that, for the sake of democracy and economic prosperity, that is, employment and exports, dogma and tradition should yield to an imaginative and farsighted use of high technology.

Technologically, it was clear that, firstly, the future of cable lay in fibre optics, but that, secondly, no system could be fully optical in the early to mid 1980s and yet, thirdly, a blend of co-axial and fibre optics was feasible and was possibly the most obvious choice. The option to use the switched-star configuration and as much optical fibre as possible might seem expensive but, said its advocates, it was not expensive if all the costs and revenues of the full futuristic service was taken into account.

Economically, the urgent imperative was to start the ball rolling by developing an audience large enough to motivate programme production so as to generate public demand for cable, both basic and pay. In the early scarcity of systems, this could be achieved by temporarily allowing low-power television stations to serve local audiences in a

Cable Television in France

fashion similar to a cable system and/or 'terrestrial
satellites', that is, transmitters using more or
less the same technology as DBS. Authorisation
would be granted, however, only to those towns
engaged in the process of cabling and signals could
be scrambled so that SLECs could work out the
subscription charges as they would for cabled
homes. The Mission Schreiner has expressed its
agreement to this policy which was first suggested
by the DGT.

Contrary to the Americans or the British, the
French were not cabling for immediate profit. The
aim was a 21st century integrated, interactive
audio-visual communication grid serving, on the
one hand, all the needs of business for data
transfer, interconnection, merchandising and sales
and, on the other hand, all the needs of
individuals for entertainment, information,
communication, education, local and national
political participation and the like. It may all be
a gamble, but a noble gamble.

NOTES

1. J.Dessaucy (March 1973) La télévision par
câble, Presse Actualité, p.56.
2. Le Monde, 4th January, 1976.
3. The number of telephones in France just
about tripled between 1975 and 1984. This required
the PTT to borrow 100 billion F (11.5 billion
dollars), half of this on the dollar market.
4. The first two broadcast in the afternoon
and the evening, the third only in the evening.
There is no morning or late night television.
5. Decisions of the Italian Supreme Court in
the mid 1970s resulted in a widespread development
of commercial radio and television stations and
networks at a huge loss to the cinema industry and
to the RAI, the public broadcasting service.
6. Its members are appointed by the President,
the Speaker of the Lower House and the President of
the Senate.
7. Le Monde, 22nd March, 1984, p.22.
8. Intermedia, May 1983, p.12.
9. H.Pigeat, (1983), La télévision par câble
commence demain, Plon, Paris, p.30.
10. S.Nora and A.Minc (1978),L'informatisation
de la société, Paris: La documentation francaise.
11. It had at the same time a 3 billion F (350
million dollar) satellite programme which was
launched in 1979. Telecom 1 was put in orbit in

161

Cable Television in France

August 1984.
    12. Intermedia, May 1983, p.14.
    13. Télédistribution Magazine, March 1984,
pp. 36-37.
    14. Presse-Actualité, February 1973, pp.
16-21.
    15. Cable could restore to the France-Musique
and France-Culture networks the sound quality which
had been much degraded by the overcrowding on the
FM band, particularly in Paris.
    16. Another advantage of cable was that the
conversion from PAL to SECAM could be done by the
cable operators.
    17. This is a satellite network which beams a
selection of programmes from francophone Belgian,
Swiss and, mainly, French television networks.
    18. A French centre for mass télématique.
Seventy thousand Minitel terminals were in use
there in early 1984.
    19. For instance, while the PTT insisted on
requiring SLECs to pay a 30 per cent advance, the
Ministry of the Interior opposed it on behalf of
the local communities.
    20. P.Flichy and G.Pineau,(eds)(1983)Images pour
le câble: Programmes et services des réseaux de
vidéocommunication, La Documentation Francaise,
Paris, p.132.
    21. H.Pigeat, (1984), Saint Écran:un âge
nouveau. La télévision par câble, Solar, Paris,
p.106.
    22. Presse-Actualité, November 1980, p.43.
    23. P.Flichy and G.Pineau, (1983), Images pour
le câble.
    24. P.Flichy (1980), Les industries de
l'imaginaire, Grenoble: Presses Universitaires de
Grenoble.
    25. H.Pigeat, (1983), La télévision par câble
commence demain, p.143.
    26. La Correspondence Municipale, May 1983,
p.3.
    27. Libération, 16th May, 1984, p.27.
    28. In May 1984, J.Chirac claimed that when
the Conservatives returned to power, they would
privatise all broadcasting except one radio and one
television network.
    29. Intermedia, May 1983, p.13. The Grandes
Écoles are graduate schools outside the university
system whose highly competitive entrance exams
require 2 to 3 years preparation after high school
graduation. They select the best students in the
country.

162

30. Le Monde, 5th May, 1984.

Chapter Six

CABLE TELEVISION IN WEST GERMANY

Michael Schacht and Rolf-Rüdiger Hoffman

THE BROADCASTING SYSTEM

The federal structure of the broadcasting system in the Federal Republic of Germany (FRG) reflects the regional organisation of post-war broadcasting. Political forces in Germany and the Western allies had wished to prevent the broadcasting system from falling under the influence of the federal government. The intention was that neither the federal government nor the federal postal service (Deutsche Bundespost) nor, indeed, private business should dominate or even influence broadcasting.

In line with the constitution, broadcasting is the cultural prerogative of the federal states, the Länder. Each broadcasting station is therefore governed either by legislation set out by one individual state when it serves one state only or by a special agreement of at least two Länder when the service crosses their borders. In 1950, all the broadcasting stations joined in the ARD (Arbeitgemein-schaft der Rundfunk-anstalten Deutschlands), the television service, which began its transmissions in 1954. At present, broadcasting is financed by a licence fee though this is supplemented by a still growing proportion of advertising revenue.

German law demands a pluralism in broadcasting so as to secure the admission of a wide range of groups, including minorities, to this very important medium of communication. But, as there was a natural scarcity of frequencies for wireless transmissions it was impossible to secure pluralism in broadcasting by licensing all groups to run their own broadcasting stations (Aussenpluralismus - a plurialism of stations differentiated by opinion). Instead, 'pluralism by organisation' (Binnenpluralismus) became one of the most important principles of the German broadcasting system.

As set out in these political aims, broadcasting stations were conceived as 'institutions of public law' (Anstalten des öffentlichen Rechts). Their duty was to represent the public interest and not any one particular single interest, and their organisation reflected this. Each broadcasting station is controlled by a council or authority which represents all relevant social groups. There are, for instance, representatives of trade unions, employers organisations, political parties, and so on. In fact, it is a legal requirement that each station have a certain number of representatives - about 30 to 40 - to form this broadcasting council (Rundfunkrat). In addition to the broadcasting council, there is also an administrative council; both councils operate in a supervisory capacity and it is 'the intendant' - a Director General - of each station who is in charge of the management of the stations.

It is, therefore, the broadcasting council, the highest body of control, which represents the public interest in broadcasting. Its duties include the setting of the budget, ensuring that programmes meet all the guidelines, supervising the management and, in the majority of stations, electing 'the intendant'.

Broadcasting has been organised, then, in such a way as to free it from any kind of state interference. The broadcasting organisations are self-administered and economically independent of the state. In practice, however, interference in programming and in matters of staffing and management by the ruling political party in the various federal states has been common. There have also been numerous debates about the choice of the 'relevant social groups' which form the broadcasting council.

Nevertheless, the system of control described above appeared to work well and it has been endorsed by many important judgements handed down by the Supreme Court. In fact, the Supreme Court has demanded that all private broadcasting services which have been made possible by the new communication technologies adopt a similar supervisory structure.

But attempts to establish private broadcasting are not new. Even before the ARD was founded, newspaper publishers in south west Germany had plans to set up their own television service. This attempt showed clearly the interest of the press in keeping up with media developments and its fear of a substantial shift in advertising revenue away from the press and to radio and television. The press was joined in these attempts by the advertising companies who were also anxious to extend their activity and their profitability. None of these attempts to establish private broadcasting systems succeeded.

Another failed attempt was the 1960 plan by the Adenauer administration to establish a national, state controlled, television service. The federal government had tried to coerce the Länder to co-operate in the Deutschland Fernsehen Gmbh by allocating the necessary investments. The Länder appealled to the Supreme Court which ruled against the federal government's attempt to influence broadcasting by setting up a new service. In this judgement, the Court laid down the main principles of the broadcasting system which are still in operation today. Broadcasting policy was seen as the responsibility of the Länder and only technical matters were judged to be outside their control. These were put under the jurisdiction of the Bundespost.

The new frequencies which were made available by the Bundespost for the second channel were allocated to the ZDF (Zweites Deutsches Fernsehen), a new nationwide television service established by the nine Länder as a centralised organisation and distribution system. In the mid 1960s, a third ARD channel was introduced. This is essentially a regional service only and has, in the past, been the producer and provider of many innovatory educational and minority programmes.

Before the present cable experiments were started, then, there were two national television services in the Federal Republic of Germany, ARD and ZDF. The regional stations contribute to the joint ARD TV service though they remain separate entities at all other times. For example, on weekdays between 6 pm and 8 pm eight groups of ARD stations transmit their own regional programmes.

Both ARD and ZDF are financed by a mixture of licence and advertising revenue. In 1982, the ARD TV stations had a revenue of £838 million ($1117), of which £650 million ($867) was from licences and £188 million ($250) from advertising. ZDF's revenue was £292 million ($389), £168 million ($165) from advertising.[1] This revenue is derived from a monthly licence fee of £4 (16.25 DM or $5.5) and advertising revenue which comes from 20 minutes block transmissions on weekdays only on both the first and second television channels.

PUBLIC BROADCASTING IN TRANSITION

In June 1981, the Supreme Court set out its guidelines for the launch of private broadcasting in Germany. This gave way to the introduction of a reformed pluralistic framework in radio and television that allowed a plurality of programme companies to represent the range of opinions inherent in German society. The Court, in effect, wanted the state parliaments to pass appropriate legislation in respect of the media so as to permit the setting up of new structures alongside the existing ones.

In its rulings, the Court forced the state parliaments to guarantee that broadcasting would be free from government interference and that the new electronic media would not be controlled or dominated by single commercial companies. Furthermore, the Court had asked for assurances that even under an open competitive system, the plurality of opinions reflected in broadcasting should be guaranteed.

The Court, in other words, made no essential distinction between broadcasting and the new electronic media of cable television or DBS. It reiterated the principles of pluralism in broadcasting that had governed the organisation of the media in Germany and it wanted these retained in the new competitive broadcasting system once the public service broadcasting monopoly was broken. But as cable television also offered a vastly greater number of channels than had ever been available previously, it was now possible to demand that the principle of plurality be guaranteed not as before by, and within, the broadcasting councils (Binnenpluralismus) but by permitting many more groups and individuals access to the medium (Aussenpluralismus - a pluralism of stations).

In practice, this still requires that state parliaments set up public control bodies, very similar to the British Independent Broadcasting Authority structure, to represent all socially relevant groups and views. So long as not all groups are represented, the state parliaments have to make sure that all programming is balanced, fair and impartial.

Following the Court's decision, the German

states began to introduce legislation for the new
media and to advertise franchises for private
broadcasting systems. In the course of the
development of local cable systems, the defenders of
public broadcasting have lost their technical
argument against a competitive and commercial
structure. Cable will effectively overcome the
scarcity of frequencies which is so basic to the
current organisation of radio and television in
Germany.

Legislation was first passed in states
governed by the Conservative CDU/CSU parties
(Christian Democrats/Christian Socialists) who have
traditionally been in favour of a free market
approach to radio and television. However, the
approaches to the new media do differ considerably
from state to state. In December 1984, Lower
Saxony, Bavaria, Rhineland-Palatinate, Saarland and
Schleswig-Holstein had passed legislation which
introduced both private cable systems and private
radio stations. Hamburg has passed a provisional
communication law which allows national satellite
programmes to be distributed on the state's cable
networks. The final law which will allow licences
to be awarded to regional and local private
broadcasters is expected in the summer of 1985.
Rhineland-Palatinate, Berlin, Bavaria and Northrhine-Westfalia have also passed laws which
regulate two-way communication as well as the
official cable television pilot projects.

The SPD (Social Democrats) had originally
fought for the integration of cable television
with the two public broadcasting systems so as to
prevent radio and television from being commercialised.
Under the pressure of technical, political and
judicial developments the SPD has changed its
approach. Now, SPD ruled states (Hamburg,
Northrhine-Westfalia and others) have introduced
legislation which aims to increase the choice for
the audience by licensing private broadcasters. The
SPD has, therefore, adhered to the principles of
securing equal access for all in the new electronic
media and the guaranteeing of internal plurality in
such systems. It is not convinced that the
economics of competition as between different
commercial broadcasters will create the plurality
of opinions in radio and television which it
desires.

All the media legislation passed so far covers
a number of common areas. It proposes the setting
up of public control boards; it attempts to secure

168

the future of the two public broadcasting organisations against private competition; there are
guidelines relating to balance in programmes and
there are others dealing with the protection of the
young; advertising is subject to certain conditions
regarding content and the maximum broadcasting time
allowed; the franchising process is explained, as
is the nature of the state's supervisory role over
the new media and there are rules governing the
use, and protection, of personal data.

There are also certain 'must carry' rules for
the cable television companies. If the number of
channels available are limited, local and regional
programme companies licensed in that specific state
have priority. Satellite programmes must be
distributed unconditionally so long as they are DBS
ones. However, they rank last if they are imported
from abroad like the German language Radio
Television Luxembourg Plus. RTL Plus is an
advertising funded service aimed at the German
audience but it is not subject to German
broadcasting legislation.

Considerations of space do not permit us to
give a detailed analysis of the highly controversial
legislation surrounding the new media. However, it
is worth looking at a number of examples of
attempts to guarantee a plurality of views on cable
television so as to ensure that the principle of
'Aussenpluralismus' (a pluralism of stations)
rather than 'Binnenpluralismus' is adhered to. Some
stations have attempted to achieve this by setting
out regulations which require a minimum number of
applicants for franchises or by laying down the
minimum number of transmission hours necessary for
each service. Such regulations, they believe, will
guarantee the plurality of ideas represented in
broadcasting under the new, and diverse, mixture of
programme providers. Furthermore, no single group
or company will be allowed to dominate the services
either economically or politically.

Schleswig-Holstein has adopted a different
position and assumes that a balance exists if there
are three private broadcasting channels additional
to the public service broadcasting ones. Bavaria
has decided to accept any group so long as they
obey the law.Hamburg will decide to award a licence
to a licensee provided that they are able to
produce at least three hours of programmes per
week. Baden Wurtemburg, however, has been
dissatisfied with the notion that the actual number
of programme providers is sufficient to engender

or guarantee pluralism. Local and state franchises
will be advertised as soon as 50 per cent of all
the households in a state are linked to cable
systems. But franchises will not be awarded until
at least 30 half-hour programmes are offered in
peak time. Furthermore, a licence will only be
awarded when at least three others can be awarded
for the same kind of radio or television service.
If the balance produced by this procedure changes,
no further licences will be awarded. Existing
franchises will then be withdrawn within three
years.

Public bodies comparable to Britain's IBA or
the proposed Cable Authority together with certain
government departments will advertise the franchises,
control the operators and have the power to
withdraw licences. Such bodies will be made up of
either representative social groups or 'honourable'
citizens acting in a voluntary capacity. The issue
of who will be represented on such bodies will be
determined by the proportional distribution of
power between the state's political parties.

Opponents of cable television are only too
ready to criticise these notions of plurality for
they deny that the state legislation can guarantee
the public control of private broadcasting as set
out by the Supreme Court. In many states, the
authorities are working very closely with the
ruling majority political party with the result
that effective public control can easily be negated
by the vested interests of the operators and
politicians.

The economics of private broadcasting is
complex. At present, all laws have been formulated
in such a way as to protect the state's traditional
media, particularly those dependent on advertising
revenue. Thus local and regional newspapers will be
protected in a number of ways. Some states forbid
local programmes funded by advertising; in other
states, only local advertising will be permitted on
local programmes. Such regulations are designed to
keep the economically powerful national media
companies and advertisers, who have no local base,
out of the local advertising market.

Spot advertising will also not be permitted.
Programmes of 100 minutes or more may, however, be
interrupted once by advertisements. Advertising on
cable will be allowed before 6 p.m. and after 8
p.m. This ruling is in direct contrast to the laws
which regulate public broadcasting. Commercial
air-time will be limited to 20 per cent of the

hour. Some regulations permit sponsorship so long as the programmes do not deal with the economic interests of the sponsors. Pay-TV and pay-per-view will be other ways which the private broadcaster can use to generate revenue.

An attempt by all Länder to harmonise their regulations regarding the distribution of satellite programmes and to allocate the German DBS service's capacity amongst themselves failed in December 1984. SPD ruled Northrhine-Westfalia refused to co-operate because the CDU/CSU states wished to freeze the amount of advertising time available for public broadcasting. Their intention here was to improve the economic prospects of the private broadcasters as against their rivals, the public broadcasting bodies.

THE CABLE EXPERIMENTS

In 1973, the federal government set up a commission of inquiry, the KtK (Kommission für den Ausbau des technischen Kommunikationsystems) to examine new developments in the fields of telecommunications. It had to consider which telecommunications services could be offered by organisations other than the existing ones and under what conditions so as to gradually expand the German telecommunications system. But, because state parliaments had sovereignty over audio-visual matters, this hindered proposals for the future development of cable television systems.

The Commission's final report was released in 1976[2] and it reflected the many interests of the electronic hardware industry, both of the Bundespost which derives the largest share of its annual revenue from its telecommunications services and private business interests looking for a quick and easy way to develop a data communication system. The attempts by newspaper publishers and other media interests to enter broadcasting were, at this stage, overlooked.

The Commission proposed that field trials should be established to test the acceptance of cable television as well as other, and different, forms of organisation and programming. There were, however, two important conditions concerning the future development of cable television. Firstly, organisations running the networks had to be clearly separate from the companies running the programming side of the operation. This condition enforced the separation of carrier and programme provider. Secondly, control over the licensing of programme operators should not be exercised by the carrier or cable operator. This condition was meant to ensure that the cable networks remain 'neutral'.

After a lengthy period of negotiations which took in such issues as private broadcasting, its social and economic consequences and the regulation of a pluralistic system, the Prime Ministers of the Länder agreed to carry out field trials in West Berlin, Dortmund (Northrhine-Westfalia), Mannheim-Ludwigshafen (Baden-Wurtemburg/Rhineland-Palatinate), and Munich (Bavaria) in 1978. All the cable networks were to be installed, and operated, by the Bundespost. Baden-Wurtemburg, however, withdrew from this plan a year later and decided to pursue independent developments in its south western region so denying the need for field trials. The decision to withdraw effectively concentrated the field trials on Ludwigshafen under the direction of Rhineland-Palatinate.

The field trials were to be accompanied by social scientific research into the acceptance of different services on offer on cable television, the social consequences of cable television and the financial and technological issues surrounding its developments generally. Proposals concerning data protection and media education are also to be drawn up.

Funding for the head-ends and the running costs of the pilot projects is to come from a surcharge of 0.20 DM (£0.05) levied on the combined radio and television licence fee. This system of funding is limited to the experimental period only. The social research into the field trials will be funded separately and paid for by the Länder.

The Ludwigshafen Trial
The Ludwigshafen project went 'on the air' on 1st January 1984. The AKK (Anstalt fur Kabelkommunikation) allocates the channels and transmission times available on the cable system to a variety of institutions, including private companies, for the provision of programmes. The controlling assembly of the AKK is supposed to reflect the plurality of all socially relevant groups in the area but as members of the AKK are not excluded from programming activities, licensees are guaranteed some influence on the board which purports to regulate them. This crucial weakness has been overcome by ensuring that the Conservative governed state of Rhineland-Palatinate has the final

adjudication over the awarding of programme
licences but for the experimental period only.
The AKK makes its decisions over the
allocation of cable time in agreement with the
programme providers. Problems of scarcity are
unlikely to emerge as the number of companies that
require full channels is, for economic reasons,
likely to be small and foreign programmers will not
be distributed automatically if they are on a low
power communications satellite. Both these factors
will ensure that there is enough space for many
programme providers. Smaller programme providers
subsequently negotiate with the AKK over the
allocation of cable time on the remaining channels.
In general, the laws governing the pilot projects
set out the conditions which have to be
fulfilled for applicants to win licences.
    The Ludwigshafen field trial covers an area of
150,000 TV households. It is still unclear whether
the required 30,000 households will be persuaded to
connect to the cable network. During the first six
months, the project has only gained about 3,500
subscribers.
    The AKK has 24 channels on offer. These
include new programmes, channels with national and
foreign programmes received in the area or brought
in via microwave links or, like the Sky Channel,
via satellite and a special full channel videotex
service.
    The ARD also feeds in an 'Open University'
service exclusive to the cable system and ZDF
presents a music channel while ZDF 2 - which is
involved in the '3 Sat' project with the public
service broadcasting systems of Austria and
Switzerland - offers a time shift channel for its
regular programmes. Among the new privately owned
broadcasting organisations is EPF (Erste Private
Fernsehgesellschaft mbH) which offers a local and
regional news service of about two hours duration
per day and PKS (Programmgesellschaft für Kabel und
Satellitenfunk) which presents a national and
international entertainment package with a news
service specially provided by the Frankfurter
Allgemeine Zeitung, a conservative quality daily
newspaper. EPF was set up by the newspaper
publishers whilst PKS - which is to be expanded and
renamed Sat 1 - was originally launched as a
consortium of banking and retail trade interests
though it now has publishers involved in it as
well. PKS is delivered by satellite. Sat 1 will
follow it in January 1985. All these services are

to be funded by advertising revenue.

The cable system also offers a channel of existing third programmes of remote ARD stations, a channel provided by clubs, organisations, churches and educational establishments and an open access channel. Pay-TV services are provided by those same organisations as are active in the British cable projects and across Europe.

Advertising is generally allowed but must be distinct from the surrounding programmes. In practice, the AKK allocates the channels without putting restrictions on the way that programme providers may generate funds for their services. However, advertising is banned on Sundays and on public holidays and, in general, it must not exceed 20 per cent of total broadcast time.

The costs of the three year trial are estimated at £18 million ($24 million). This comprises £13 million ($17.3 million) for investment and £5 million ($6.6 milliion) for the trial's running costs. Cable subscribers are charged a £100 ($133) connection charge and a monthly fee of £1.25 ($1.60).As always, premium pay-TV channel will have to be paid for separately. Such services are due to start in January 1985 and so far only three have been established. These will include two film channels and one games channel. A cabletext service is also being proposed for the future.

Munich

On April 1st 1984, the second cable experiment was launched in Munich. This project is run by a limited company which is responsible for the allocation of channels, the central head-end and the studio complex. Its shareholders include the Bavarian public broadcasting station (10 per cent), the second public television service (10 per cent), the state (20 per cent), the chambers of commerce and trade (10 per cent), the Bavarian publishing companies (20 per cent), and the audio-visual production companies of Bavaria (20 per cent). Originally, the City of Munich also had a 10 per cent share in the company but the Social Democratic Council of the City decided for political reasons, to withdraw its support in May 1984. Like the other field trials, it is the Bundespost which runs the cable network. A separate private company has also been set up to market the project.

The Bavarian constitution insists that only the two public broadcasting companies have responsibility for radio and television services. Private

Cable Television in West Germany

radio and television broadcasting companies have to
comply with this requirement and so rely on the
editorial decisions of ARD and ZDF. Since cable and
teletext services are considered to be different
from broadcasting, responsibility for their
services has been devolved to the cable company.
About 50,000 households lie within the
boundary of the field trial. By August 1984, 5,700
households were connected to the network and it is
hoped that in the next three years between 10,000
and 15,000 will take part.
The 24 channel tree and branch network carries
the following services: all terrestrial public
television channels, the Austrian and Swiss public
television channels, some distant German regional
channels, Music Box, the Sky Channel, French TV 5,
the commercial PKS channel, the ZDF cable music
service and two local channels. These local
channels show a range of cultural, entertainment,
educational and sports programmes produced by the
Bavarian public broadcasting service in collaboration
with private programme providers.
In 1985, it is hoped to add two film channels
and a games channel. Other local services will be
provided in 1985. Twenty four radio channels, some
of them provided exclusively for cable, are also
available as is a cabletext channel run by German
newspaper publishers.
Subscribers are charged a monthly fee of £4.75
($6.3). Programme providers have to pay a secondary
rental charge to the cable company and they finance
their programme services either through advertisements
or through some form of pay-TV.
Some weeks prior to the launch of the project,
the Bavarian government introduced legislation
covering the whole range of electronic media which
were likely to break the monopoly of the public
broadcasting organisations. Over the years the
ruling Bavarian Christian Social Union (CSU) had
put political pressure on its public broadcasting
system in order to try and get better coverage of
its opinions in all programmes. With the new
legislation passed in the Bavarian parliament in
October 1984, the CSU will strengthen its grip on
the electronic media in Bavaria.
The new public 'Cable Authority', for example,
will be made up of members of the Bavarian
parliament with the CSU in the majority. Also
represented on that body will be members of the
state government and a number of groups deemed
socially relevant by the state government and
parliament. This public authority will license and

control private cable broadcasters in Bavaria and in competition with ARD and ZDF. Contrary to the notion of the independence of broadcasting from state interference, all Bavarian community councils will have the right to see their own local programmes distributed on cable with only the political broadcasts prohibited.

In January 1986, the Munich experiment will be extended to cover all of Bavaria so as to make private broadcasting economically viable. This expansion will take place irrespective of the results of the social and economic research which is accompanying the field trials.

Berlin
The third cable television field trial will be launched in September 1985. Within the subsequent five years, the Berlin government wants to gain enough experience to develop a long term strategy for the co-existence of the print and electronic media. But for the duration of the trial, it will award franchises to both public and private broadcasting organisations.

The 200,000 households already connected to cable systems in Berlin are free to decide whether they wish to take part in the project. If they opt out, they will still have access to the existing programmes on cable - ARD, ZDF, SFB, DDR 1 and 2 and the three Forces Networks - supplemented by DBS channels. Taking part in the experiment will, however, give them access to extra local channels as well as some public or private, national or foreign satellite programmes. This second tier of programmes will be additional to the basic service.

For the first experimental period, the programmes transmitted will be free. After two and a half years, basic and other fees will be charged. The main reason for the postponment of payments is to let householders learn as much as possible about the new services free of charge. It is then hoped that they will be in a better position to decide whether to subscribe or not. All the services - except pay-TV proper - will be available in an unscrambled form during the first two and a half years. Eventually, programmes will be available to subscribers on either a pay-TV or pay-per-view basis.

The experiment will also carry open access channels in which individuals and social groups will have the opportunity to make their views and opinions known. The licensing authority hopes to

176

set aside 20 hours per week for this purpose and the service will be financed and technically supported by the cable company. Responsibility for the open channels will lie with either the public broadcasting companies or private associations specially set up for this task.

Originally, it was also hoped that the Berlin experiment would develop new types of services and programme content but for a variety of economic reasons nearly all of these plans have been abandoned. Publishers in Berlin had also refused to broadcast their own programmes so long as the originally envisaged mandatory scambling procedure was likely to create audiences too small to generate advertising funds. However, political pressure from the publishers changed the project's design in favour of the free introductory period described above. In any case, local advertising is severely restricted on cable services as a means of protecting the local print media.

To guarantee a measure of public control, a public 'Cable Authority' will be set up. But in contrast to the Bavarian model, members of governments and parliaments and representatives of programme companies will be excluded from its board. The Authority's role will be to allocate the franchises, control the programme companies and distribute the channels. The cable system will be run by the Bundespost and a private limited company supervised by the Authority will administer the technical side of the project and allocate transmission times.

The Authority will have the right to withdraw franchises, restrict transmission times or postpone a licence if it decides that a programme provider has breached the guidelines. Furthermore, a special committee will be formed to exercise a degree of self-regulation so as to avoid the full sanctions of the Authority in case of possible complaints about programme content. This committee will consist of three representatives of private broadcasters, three members of the cable company and one member each of the Berlin government and the 'Cable Authority' and a representative from the 'protection of youth' bodies.

The project will be funded out of public funds, licence fees and levies to be paid by the programme companies.

Dortmund
The Northrhine-Westfalia project is the only one

which is the sole responsibility of an ARD
broadcasting organisation (WDR - Westdeutscher
Rundfunk). It is likely to start in June 1985.
Private broadcasters will not be allowed to take
part in this project and commercial advertising
will also be prohibited.

The Dortmund network will carry all channels
already available in the area, new local channels,
an open access channel, the ZDF music channel, a
cabletext magazine, city technical services such as
electricity and 11 two-way channels. WDR also
intends to offer its own pay-TV services consisting
of special interest programmes and material from
its library. It will also test different methods of
payment - pay-per-view as opposed to pay-per-channel
- to guage the subscribers' responses.

Not all these services will be available to
prospective subscribers. The project area covers an
inner district of Dortmund with about 37,000 TV
households though only 10,000 are supposed to take
part in the government subsidised field trials.
They will all have access to the broadcast channels
but only 3000 will have access to the cabletext
service and only 600 will be linked to two-way
services and an extra narrowband feedback channel.
These elements - feedback, narrowcasting and new
local technical services - are unique to the
Dortmund project. The total cost of the three year
project are estimated in the region of £23 million
($30 million). This includes investment costs,
running costs and marketing but not programming
costs.

To supervise the project and its programmes, a
project council has been established. Members of
this council were elected by the parliament of
Northrhine-Westfalia and the Dortmund city council.
Viewers and listeners from Dortmund also have seats
on the council.

TOMORROW'S TELEVISION

The media legislation passed by the state
parliaments has made all the cable experiments of
little significance. However, they will still go
ahead. Irrespective of the findings, private
commercial broadcasting and cable television will
dominate the future development of German mass
communication.

With the move to the Conservatives in the
German federal government, the Bundespost has
speeded up the construction of an infrastructure

178

for private cable television systems. Today, the Bundespost is investing about £250 million ($333 million) per annum in order to lay a national, tree and branch, cable system. It is expected that by the mid 1990s almost 60 per cent of all households will be passed by cable systems. At present, about 1.8 million households are passed by cable with 600,000 of them connected to cable systems which relay existing terrestrial programmes.

To raise additional funds, the Bundespost intends to co-operate with local councils and cable companies. This will complement its own self-financed cabling of the country. Such newly formed companies will, between them, share the installation, running and marketing costs of the cable system. The Post Office will take 24.9 per cent of all the shares and the rest will be divided equally between the local councils, cable and electronic manufacturers, local newspapers and programme companies. If granted by the Post Office an exclusive contract of 12 years duration, these companies will be required to, firstly, cable the franchise areas starting at the Post Office distribution points and, secondly, sell the cable connections to the householder. In return, the Post Office will claim a 50 per cent share of the joint companies' revenue. The cities of Wolfsburg and Braunschweig in Lower Saxony are the first to go ahead with this scheme.

This financial structure is not particularly conducive and many private companies and local councils have hesitated rather than commit themselves to the expensive process of laying cable systems. But with the states' media legislation currently in force, channels that are not ordinarily available off-air may be made available to potential cable subscribers and this is seen by the cable companies as a possible incentive to cable an area that will generate funds.

Housing corporations are proving to be a key factor in cable's penetration. If they decide to connect their buildings, their tenants can hardly avoid being connected to the system although they retain the right to decide whether they wish to use their cable socket as part of a community antenna system or wish to pay for additional programming.

Market research indicates that not more than one third of German television households want more programmes. Films, entertainment and sports channels are the firm favourites of those who do. But there is a reluctance to pay for these extra services; 20 per cent of those who wish to gain

access to extra channels are not happy to pay
another licence fee and only 9 per cent of those
people interested in cable are prepared to pay £5
($6.5) per month on top of the regular television
licence fee of £4 ($5.5) per month.

The real financial burden the cable householder
will have to bear is, of course, much greater.
Firstly, for the privilege of being connected to
the cable network, the householder has to pay the
Post Office £60 ($80) and £1.50 ($2) per month
depending on the number of channels received. From
1985 onwards, these sums will be increased to £125
($166) and £2.25 ($3) respectively. For the first
year only, the Post Office is due to advertise a
special offer for blocks of flats so as to increase
penetration. It may reduce the connection charge to
about £20 (about £26.6) depending on the number of
flats connected. Secondly, the Post Office is not
responsible for the cable installation in the home.
To get the cable socket ready to plug in, the
householder has to pay at least another £50 ($65)
to a private antenna company. If a housing
corporation takes on this responsibility, then the
householder pays this fee in monthly installments
of about £5 ($6.5).

Thirdly, the majority of television sets are
not designed for cable. The householder needs a
converter: £70 ($93) for a cable television set
tuner or £125 ($166) for a converter and decoder to
unscramble pay-TV channels. Finally, if a joint
cable company steps in in between the Post Office
and an antenna company, the householder may have to
pay a further £5 ($6.5) per month for the company's
additional, second tier programmes. Pay channels
will cost an extra £6 ($8) to £8 ($10.6) per month.

In these circumstances, broadcasters and the
advertising industry are wondering precisely how
much householders will be prepared to pay for their
cable television services. As funds are always
limited only a few national and multinational media
conglomerates will be able to compete with the high
quality of the existing German public service
broadcasting institutions. There will be a few
niches for local programme makers but they will
also have to fight for their own survival.

But changes in the German media system are
also partly influenced by forces from outside the
German multimedia, most notably from satellite
transmissions. The German multimedia giant
Bertelsmann has joined forces with the private
Radio Tele Luxembourg (RTL) to launch its new

German TV channel, RTL Plus. This is now aimed at an audience of 1.3 million in the south west but from 1986 onwards this service will also be distributed by the French TDF DBS service which will make it available across all of Germany either directly or when relayed by cable.

RTL's commercial channel attracts its audience with a mixture of easy viewing popular programmes and cheap imports, a formula used by Radio Luxembourg since 1958. With production costs at only £40 to £50 (about $60) or only 3 per cent of comparable ARD costs, large profits are expected. The joint venture with Bertelsmann demonstrates how German media organisations are keen to find profitable arrangements in foreign media markets so as to evade the restrictions imposed by German law.

Two channels of the European Communications Satellite (ECS) are also leased to the Bundespost for satellite broadcasting. By agreement of the prime ministers of the Länder in February 1984, the ECS East beam was given over to the ZDF time shift service. The German language television services of Austria and Switzerland have joined the ZDF for the joint '3 Sat' programme service which was launched in December 1984. The West beam was given over to Sat 1, a private consortium formed by major companies in Germany, such as the Springer, Bauer and Burda groups. Sixty per cent of the programming will be provided by PKS. It will be funded by advertisements.

The programme schedule of the private service will consist of entertainment, films and series interrupted by a daily news show and regional items. The news service will be supplied by the Aktuell Presse Fernsehen (APF), a joint venture of 165 publishing houses of which the Springer group is the largest shareholder. To survive commercially it clearly has to aim at a broader audience than will be reached by any of the field trials. The Bertelsmann group was excluded from this consortium because of its share in the competing RTL Plus service.

From 1985 onwards, the Bundespost will make available another six channels via Intelsat V and a national satellite to be launched in 1987 will expand the system by a further seven channels. As always, it will remain the prerogative of the Länder to decide on how to dispose of these channels.

With the media laws passed, every Länd will have to advertise at least one new terrestrial

frequency for private radio. The major publishing
houses have already started to apply for these
licences in the belief that large profits are to be
made. For example, Bertelsmann together with Radio
Luxembourg and Neue Constantin, the film production
and distribution company, hope to provide networked
programmes (including commercials) to all of
Germany's independent radio stations. Bertelsmann
will, however, also apply for its own licences. The
Springer group has joined the film distributor
which is backing PKS for the supply of radio
programmes and Burda, another major publishing
group, has joined up with the German Music Box
Video channel to supply radio services. Burda is
also expected to co-operate with Springer.

In addition to these groupings, middle sized
publishing groups have also formed radio consortia
in numerous Länder. Because of the guarantees for
pluralism that are being asked for, it is likely
that some of these ventures will succeed to the
disadvantage of the many other, private and
alternative, groups which seem to lack political
backing.

In this rapidly changing media environment,
two major criticisms which have been voiced raise
serious doubts about the direction, and benefit, of
the present trends. One of these criticisms has
concentrated on the technological side of cable
television developments, whilst the other has
focussed on the impact of change on the existing
broadcasting services.

Critics of the Bundespost have often argued
that it is economically and technologically
wasteful to install the traditional co-axial tree
and branch configuration for the distribution of
television services only. Their major point is that
a real demand for more television has yet to be
demonstrated. To make the German electronic
industry more competitive internationally, their
argument proceeds, all services of individual and
mass communication need to be integrated into a
single digital optical network. Indeed, in order to
meet the changes brought about by the increasing
computerisation of office communication, the
Bundespost should be pressed to develop a universal
broadband telecommunications network which uses
optical fibres.[3]

Although the Bundespost is presently running
seven experiments with optical fibres so as to test
the technical integration of data and telecommunications, it has so far refused to develop a single

optical network without having any proof that a
demand actually exists. But, at the same time, it
has agreed to go ahead with co-axial cables so as
to satisfy what it sees as the growing demand for
more television programmes. As far as the Post
Office is concerned, a demand for cable can only
increase if there is more programming available.

To break through the limits of the tree and
branch system, the Post Office proposes to connect
cable households to an individually addressable
system which contains the option for a narrowband
return channel. Because the cost of this sytem is
in the region of £600 ($800) per household, private
broadcasters fear that it would delay even further
cable's penetration. Within the field trials,
scrambling devices will be used to obtain scrambled
services rather than the more advanced technological
instruments currently available.

The danger in all this is that Germany may be
landed with a crude, unsophisticated and rather
restrictive technology instead of the more advanced
technology currently being developed.

The other criticism that is voiced is
concerned with the changes to the broadcasting
system that the present trends may bring about.
Many have expressed concern that the broadcasting
system is in danger of losing its function as an
important source of objective political information
for the public since only the financially strong
media companies will be able to take part in the
new media world. Economic power, in other words,
may soon come to dominate broadcasting.

There are also signs that the impending
changes and the increase in the number of channels
of entertainment television are having an effect on
the existing public service organisations. After an
initial period of hesitation, the ARD and ZDF have
started to fight back against their private
competitors. Their now aggressive strategy has many
parts to it. Not only have they demanded equivalent
financial support for the development of their own
cable television and satellite services but they
have also begun to make their programme schedules
more popular. There are even plans, for example, to
change the television news programmes into more
entertaining news shows. Both the ARD and ZDF have
also invested heavily in the purchase of popular
films. With their eyes on the ratings, they have
each spent about £65 million ($86 million) to
secure the rights to some 1300, mainly American,
films many of which have never been seen on German

television. Furthermore, they have attempted to lower production costs by dispersing productions to private companies, some of whom take sponsorship.
The strategy of the public broadcasting services is obvious. Using their considerable financial strength, they are trying to push back private competition even before it has actually started. No private broadcaster can expect to make any profit during the next five years and only a few will have the financial resources to survive in an advertising market that is likely to be large enough for one, or perhaps two, national television channels. But, in this atmosphere of increased competition for the audiences, and in effect the commercialisation of broadcasting, it may be that the quality, standards and plurality of the system that has for so long characterised German broadcasting is sacrificed for ratings and profit.

NOTES

1. The rates of exchange in January 1985 were as follows: £1 = 4 DM, $1 = 3 DM (approximately).
2. Kommission für den Ausbau des technischen Kommunikationssystems (KtK), Telekommunikationsbericht, Bonn.
3. SCS (ed) (1984), SCS-Studie zur künftigen Entwicklung der öffentlichen fernmeldenetze in der BRD und ihre Auswirkungen auf die Benutzer, Hamburg.

REFERENCES

Other texts relevant to the 'new media' in Germany include:

S.Huth and P.Löhr (1982), Kabelfernsehen: Eine Bibliographie. Konzepte, Projekte, Erfahrungen, Muchen-New York-London.
B.P. Lange (1980), Kommerzielle Ziele und binnen pluralistiche Organisation bei Rundfunkveranstaltern. Eine Untersuchung aus wirtschaftswissenschaftlicher und kommunikationstheoretischer Sicht, Frankfurt am Main, Berlin.
Media Perspektiven (1984),Daten zur Mediensituation in der Bundescrepublik 1983, Frankfurt am Main.
H.Montag (1978), Privater oder öffentlich-recht-licher Rundfunk?Initiativen für einen privaten Rundfunk in der Bundesrepublik, Berlin.

Cable Television in West Germany

D.Ratzie (1982), Handbuch der Neuen Medien, Stuttgart.
M.Schmidbauer and P.Löhr (1983), Die Kabelpilotprojekte in der Bundesrepublik Deutschland. Ein Hanbbuch, München-New York-London.
E.Wittich (1983), Communication policy in the Federal Republic of Germany: Democratic Expectations versus Political and Economic Interests, in P.Edgar and S.Rahim (eds.) (1983), Communication Policy in Developed Countries, London-Boston-Melbourne.

Chapter Seven

CABLE TELEVISION IN AUSTRALIA: A STUDY OF REPOSE

Geoffrey Caldwell

This is a chapter about cable television in Australia, when in fact, Australia does not have cable television, nor is there any immediate or apparent plans to introduce cable television. However, during 1980-82, a major inquiry into this question was conducted by the Australian Broadcasting Tribunal, the major controlling body in Australian broadcasting.

This chapter will be concerned with two matters. First, a description of the Tribunal's Inquiry into cable television and radiated subscription television services; and, second, reasons will be offered for the state of repose on the cable television issue.

In mid 1980, the Minister for Post and Communications in the Australian Federal Government directed the Australian Broadcasting Tribunal to conduct an inquiry into the introduction of cable and subscription television services into Australia and to make appropriate recommendations. The report was issued in 1982, and its major recommendation was 'that Australia introduce cable television services (CTV) and radiated subscription television services (RSTV) as soon as practicable'. Despite the Australian Broadcasting Tribunal's endorsement of cable television, no additional steps have been taken since then to bring cable television to the Australian communications scene.

THE AUSTRALIAN BROADCASTING TRIBUNAL'S INQUIRY INTO CABLE AND SUBSCRIPTION TELEVISION SERVICES FOR AUSTRALIA

Terms of Reference
The Inquiry was directed by the Minister for Posts and Telecommunications, Mr A.A. Staley, to make

recommendations upon the following:

1. the social, economic, technical, and related matters that need to be taken into account in introducing cable television into Australia;
2. the range and diversity of services (including sound broadcasting and pay-TV and other subscription services) of an entertainment, information, educational or other kind that could be provided by means of, or in association with, cable television;
3. the level of interest of potential operators in providing services of the kind referred to in paragraph (2) above, and of potential consumers in receiving such services;
4. the means by which potential operators would propose to establish and operate systems for the provision of cable television and associated services;
5. optimum dates for the introduction of cable television, having regard to the present state of development of cable technology, including fibre optics;
6. the effect that the introduction of radiated 'Subscription Television' services would be likely to have on any pay-TV services provided by cable television systems;
7. the effect of the introduction of cable television on existing broadcasting and television services, including any effect on the viability of commercial broadcasting stations and commercial television stations;
8. the effect of the introduction of cable television on the production in Australia of programmes, films and other material designed or suitable for television, and the employment of persons in connection therewith;
9. whether any private operators of cable television systems that might be permitted should be subject to licensing, ownership and control, and other regulatory requirements of the kind that apply in relation to commercial broadcasting stations and commercial television stations or, alternatively, whether other provisions should be made in relation to those matters;

10. whether any private operators of cable television systems that might be permitted should be subject to requirements relating to the Australian content of programmes or the provisions of channels for community services, public access services or special purpose programmes, or subject to other special requirements;
11. the copyright and related issues to which the introduction of cable television would give rise;
12. the means by which the 'hardware' (including ducts, cables and associated equipment) necessary for the establishment and operation of cable television systems might be provided and the means by which participation by Australian industry in the provision, manufacture, installation and servicing of the necessary equipment might be maximised.[1]

It is curious and perhaps indicative, to note that just 6 months later, the new Minister holding the relevant portfolio, Communications, Mr Ian Sinclair, made some changes in the terms of reference. The most important change was that requiring the Tribunal to address the question of whether cable television and/or pay-television services distributed by cable should or should not be introduced in Australia, and to comment on the potential roles and purposes of any such services in considering whether and how they might be introduced. The Minister also requested the Tribunal, while considering the possible roles and purposes of cable and pay-television, to identify the non broadcasting services which might be provided by this means, and the issues associated with those services.[2]

In the first volume of its five volume report, the Inquiry defined some broad objectives for the Australian Broadcasting System. Such a system should consist of a number of sectors that involve and utilise, to varying degrees and in different ways, private and public ownership and participation; be economically and administratively viable in its various sectors and as a total system; be sufficiently flexible, dynamic, enterprising and diverse to respond to the wide range of changing needs implicit within the complexities of Australian society; be effectively owned and controlled by Australians and ensure that ownership of the system

188

and control of the provision of programme services is spread as widely as practicable throughout the Australian community; enable the various sectors to complement each other in the provision of programme services avoiding as far as practicable, unnecessary and wasteful duplication of broadcasting facilities, resources and content; provide programme services efficiently and economically.

Further the Tribunal stated that programme services should be of a high standard; would inform, educate and entertain; contribute to a sense of national identity; provide reasonable, balanced opportunity for the free expression of differing views on matters of public concern; cater for, and reflect, the widest possible spectrum of information, opinions, values, and interests in Australian society; use Australian creative and other resources; and safeguard, enrich and strengthen the cultural, political, social and economic fabric of Australia.

Such a system should provide programme services throughout Australia for all people who require those services - within reasonable limits of practicality; the broadcasting system should provide regulation and supervision of the system with appropriate adaptiveness and flexibility to adjust to changes in technology and Australian society.[3]

SPECIFIC OBJECTIVES FOR CABLE TELEVISION

Moreover the Inquiry spelled out specific objectives for CTV and RSTV sectors. For example, CTV and RSTV should:

- Further the attainment of the broad objectives for the Australian Broadcasting System to the maximum extent that their particular characteristics permit.
- Ensure that ownership of the System and control of the provision of programme services is spread as widely as practicable throughout the Australian community by extending and broadening the opportunity for participation.
- Plan, establish, maintain and operate CTV and RSTV in such a way that they will be compatible with existing sectors of, and likely future developments in, the Australian Broadcasting System.

- Preserve the viability of the other
  sectors of the Australian Broadcasting
  System and in particular to protect the
  economic viability of commercial broadcasters
  (radio and television) to the extent
  necessary to enable such broadcasters to
  discharge their responsibilities to the
  communities they are licensed to serve.
- As far as practicable:
  (a) to encourage the provision of pro-
      grammes wholly or substantially
      produced in Australia and to use
      Australians in the presentation of
      programmes on CTV and RSTV as well as
      the establishment, maintenance and
      operation of CTV and RSTV;
  (b) to utilise Australian industry and
      technology in the establishment,
      maintenance and operation of CTV and
      RSTV and thereby facilitate the
      development and experience of
      Australian industry in these
      technologies.
- To plan, establish and operate CTV and
  RSTV to:
  (a) utilise available technology efficiently
      and economically compatible with
      likely future developments in tech-
      nology;
  (b) to meet the specific needs of
      particular communities or geographic
      areas having regard to their economic,
      social and other characteristics.
- Make the services provided by these
  sectors available throughout Australia on
  the basis of a direct consumer payment for
  all people who reasonably require those
  services and who can be realistically
  served.
- To integrate the regulation and supervision
  of CTV and RSTV with the other sectors of
  the Australian Broadcasting System.[4]

In addition the Inquiry had some special
objectives for the cable television sector which
were:
- To utilise the multiple channel capacity
  of CTV to provide programme services
  designed to cater for a wide range of
  specialised interests within Australian
  society.

190

- To utilise the multiple channel capacity
  of CTV to enable members of communities
  and community groups to participate in and
  provide programme services that cater for
  the interests of a particular community,
  or communities, and to provide greater
  opportunity for the members of communities
  to express differing views on matters of
  public concern and generally discuss and
  debate local issues and events.
- To provide, as far as practicable, greater
  and more diverse opportunities for the
  promotion and advertising of goods and
  services and the dissemination of community
  service information.
- To plan, establish, maintain, operate and
  regulate CTV in such a way as to ensure
  that the convergence of entertainment,
  information and communications technologies
  is not inhibited and that the ability of
  CTV to meet private and commercial needs
  for communication services is appropriately
  utilised.[5]

The report covers 77 recommendations and its
work runs into five volumes (with a sixth
consisting mainly of conclusions and recommendations)
containing technical papers, commissioned social,
economic and education studies, international
papers, survey results, Tribunal research studies
and demand studies. Despite the fact that the
Tribunal's conclusions endorsed the introduction of
cable television as soon as practicable, there has
been a deathly silence on the cable television
issue since the report's circulation.

REASONS FOR THE DECLINE OF INTEREST IN CABLE
TELEVISION

Some 6 months after the publication of the report,
a Federal election was called and held in March
1983. The Liberal National Party coalition was
defeated and the Labour government which had been
dismissed in 1975 assumed power. The new government
has simply shelved the issue and shows no
enthusiasm for considering the introduction of
cable television.
    Nor does there seem to have been much outcry
about the apparent abandonment by the government on
the issue - apart from a couple of newspaper
articles. For example, Douglas[6] has argued that the

Liberal National Government which was defeated in
the 1983 election left the Labour Government with a
large number of unresolved communication policy
issues, even though it was clearly inclined to
believe that private enterprise should be given the
opportunity to find a way out of the mess. The
Labour Government has been much less ready to
sympathise with such a view, particularly as it
would create a competitive conflict with the
existing common carrier, Telecom. Douglas also
points out that there have never been so many
complex problems affecting broadcasting and
telecommunications, converging simultaneously as is
the case now. He spoke of the promise of cable
television not in terms of its interactive capacity
but in terms of its programming diversity as well
as its job generation potential and laments the
'very quiet' performance of the Australian Cable
and Subscription Communications Association, which
was formed to press for the introduction of cable
and subscription television.[7]

THE VIDEOCASSETTE RECORDER REVOLUTION IN AUSTRALIA

Given that the labour Government is not interested
in the introduction of cable television and there
has been no public outcry, what accounts for this
almost complete disinterest? The answer almost
certainly lies in the widespread diffusion of the
videocassette recorder. In a report to the
Australian Broadcasting Tribunal's Inquiry in which
I explored the likely sociological impact of CTV
and RSTV, I predicted that in the field of
telecommunications there would be a 'growing and
substantial use of VCRs within Australia'.[8] A
number of newspaper articles have testified to the
high penetration of VCRs - in as many as a third of
Australian homes. Just as Australians embraced
black and white and then colour television, so the
evidence is accumulating that Australians are
adopting VCRs with the same enthusiasm.

In all parts of Australia a new industry has
been established. In service stations, newsagents,
department stores and speciality shops, video
movies are hired out. Perhaps it is a symbol of the
times that the movie hire shops recall the local
lending library though their wares are audio-visual,
not books. Such a swing to the videocassette
recorder, it would seem, is also happening in the
United States, which unlike Australia, has
considerable experience of cable television. Time

magazine reports that VCRs are producing an entertainment revolution and changing the habits of the US, and that the VCR has proved to be the most vigorous of the video delivery systems that emerged in the 1970s. It continues:

> Cable envisioned dozens of specialised channels that would satisfy virtually every individual needs or taste. But the promise dimmed as the financial realities of such eclectic programming sank in: viewers and advertisers, so far at least, have not been able to support more than a handful of cable networks offering mass-audience fare little different from that of the big three networks.[9]

'Time' magazine also suggests that the 'VCR seems to be the right product at the right time'. If that is the case with the United States, it is even more relevant in Australia. In the United States cable television preceded the growing diffusion of VCRs. In Australia VCRs have come first. It can be stated with a great degree of confidence that cable television will not come to Australia before the 1990s, unless there are very powerful advocates, promoters and entrepreneurs. If such entrepreneurs exist, they are adopting a very low profile, and they are making little or no attempt to persuade Australians of the virtues of cable television.

In my sociological impact report to the ABT's Inquiry on CTV and RSTV, I included the following paragraphs:

> I can remember reading in a newspaper about an Australian in London during the early 1960s, who complained as the permissive age began to emerge, that he didn't have enough time (and energy?) to follow up all the leads, so busy was he with available sexual opportunities.
> Perhaps by the time cable TV is introduced into Australia, there will not be enough time (and energy?) to follow up all the entertainment and communication opportunities that will be available - given the availability of VCRs, satellites, videotext and possibly RSTV and cable television. As this researcher has worked through the possible effects of these technologies, one is left with the impression of a surfeit of new technological and telecommunications developments.[10]

It can be concluded then that Australia with its limited population size of fifteen million and less than a dozen cities of significant size, is very unlikely to become a cable TV country before the 1990s. Such a prediction is based on the assumption that VCRs and computers are the new communication/ technology toys. Once Australians have become used to VCRs as part of the accepted telecommunications package, only then may they be receptive to any new technology such as cable television. Because VCRs allow individuals to time-shift, hire movies, tape programmes for later or repeated viewings, record family events with the aid of a camera, watch and record simultaneously, they are permitting a considerable expansion in programme diversity and individual discretion over viewing patterns. Thus, some of the powerful attractions of cable TV are, to a considerable extent, being satisfied by VCRs. At the present time, the interactive capacity of cable television is hardly appreciated within the Australian context. Before its capacity is understood and appreciated, Australians will have to have much greater experience of home and work computers - a process which has only just begun in Australia.

In summary then, contemporary Australians seem to be largely content with the entertainment provided through the television set and the videocassette recorder. It can be anticipated that once the novelty of VCRs have worn off, and computers have been more widely experienced by the Australian population, interest in the interactive capacity of cable television might accelerate. Entrepreneurs will watch closely the experience of cable television in the United States, before taking any further steps to try and introduce cable television into Australia. Consumers and providers seem to have jointly reached the conclusion that the time is not ripe for the introduction of cable television into Australia. Furthermore, attention is being diverted to Aussat - Australian's Telecommunications Satellite to be sent aloft in 1985. It may well be true that Australia with its large spread of viewers may be much better suited to satellite transmission than cable because it can provide as many signals in regional and remote areas as in cities.

NOTES

1. Australian Broadcasting Tribunal, August 1982, Cable and Subscription Television Services for Australia. Main conclusions and Recommendations, pp.4-5.
2. Australian Broadcasting Tribunal, August 1982, p.6.
3. Australian Broadcasting Tribunal, August 1982, pp. 23-24.
4. Australian Broadcasting Tribunal, August 1982, pp. 25-26.
5. Australian Broadcasting Tribunal, August 1982, p.26.
6. H.Douglas, 1983, 'Pay-TV plans cause conflict', The Australian, June 28, 1983. Also, 'Future of Cable TV in balance', The Australian, July 12, 1983.
7. H.Douglas, 1983, 'Time to give thought to technology', The Australian, July 19, 1983.
8. G.Caldwell, 1982, 'The likely sociological impact of radiated subscription and cable television' in Australian Broadcasting Tribunal, August 1982, Report, Volume 5: Social, Economic and Education Studies, p.115.
9. Time Magazine, 1984, 'VCRs: Coming on strong', December 24, 1984, p.51.
10. G.Caldwell, 1982, pp.123-124.

Chapter Eight

TELEVISION AND CABLE POLICY IN JAPAN: AN ESSAY

Michael Tracey

We have in Britain, and perhaps in Europe also, become totally enamoured of the idea that whatever the future of television in an economic or organisational sense, and therefore in terms of programming, cable television and satellite television will be an important part of the final mix. One cannot hold a conversation now about the future of broadcasting without it quickly becoming a conversation about the future of cable and satellite.

Elsewhere in this volume the issue of the distinctions between the hype about cable and its economic and social realities, and the question marks against the financial prospects for cable TV, are raised. It would, however, be true to say that it is widely assumed that something extremely important is happening to the landscape of audio-visual culture within these countries, even if the configuration which is emerging remains unknown and unknowable.

The interesting feature which strikes the European observer of communications policies in Japan is how different the tone and quality of the discussion about the future of broadband cable actually is and of the relative lack of interest in cable TV developments as sources of entertainment. What does stand out is the crucial development of policy to deal with the role of a cable infrastructure in the creation of an information society. What I want to argue in this essay is that in Japan cable TV will, for the foreseeable future, have little effect on the state of broadcast culture; that there is a considerable level of satisfaction with the status quo and no great demand for more entertainment services on the part of the audience, and that the really important

196

aspect of cable which has aroused massive interest there are its telecommunications potentialities.

Much has been made in the United States and Britain of the fact that cable could deliver a considerable increase in the number of entertainment channels that could be offered to the television audience. Ludicrous figures of 200 channels were offered as an ostensible inducement to franchise awarders in the US. In Britain and across the rest of Europe we were to be tempted with all kinds of goodies of films, culture, sport, news and comment, a veritable feast of television. We can now see that it was all oversold, that the public neither wanted nor, more importantly, was willing to pay for such extravagance and that the star of cable has in the past twelve months dimmed considerably. Nevertheless policy on cable in, for example, Britain (see chapter 4 above) plods on, employing the same basic logic: entertainment services will lead us into the future of the information society, even if that means that certain changes must take place in the nature and organisation of the existing broadcasting service. To be blunt, NHK, the Japanese public service broadcasting organisation, is more likely to remain virgo intacto than the BBC.

There is, of course, some interest in developing cable TV as a new source of entertainment among industrial concerns in Japan - beguiled rather in the manner that British companies were in the first instance by the message which seemed to be emerging from the United States about the considerable amounts of money to be had through pay-TV. this has not however captured either the popular or official imagination to anything like the extent to which it has in Britain and elsewhere. What has occurred is an increasing sense of the need to de-regulate telecommunications services, at the same time as vastly increasing the kinds and numbers of services available, while using the power and influence of the state to ensure that the future of telecommunications and information infrastructures in Japan are adequately developed to meet with the needs of the post-industrial society. Comparing Japanese policy-making on new communications systems and those in Britain is a bit like comparing the tightly organised routines of American football with the amateurish and planned chaos of the Eton wall game.

In Britain the culture of television as traditionally understood has become inextricably

linked   with   the   development   of   cable   and
telecommunications   policy.   In   Japan   television
policy remains to a much greater extent separate.Let
me   first   of   all   describe   some   of   the   key   features
of   the   culture   of   broadcasting   in   Japan   -   its
institutions,   laws,   programming,   audience   and   then
consider   the   kinds   of   policies   about   new
communications   which   are   being   developed.   The   point
which   emerges   is   that   in   the   whole   they   do   not
intersect.

Japanese   broadcasting   was   to   an   extent   born
out   of   national   disaster.   In   1923   Tokyo   was
devastated   by   a   major   earthquake,   which   not   only
damaged   property   and   caused   a   vast   loss   of   life,
but   also   severely   ruptured   all   forms   of   communication
with   the   outside   world.   All   that   is   except   one,
radio.   The   quake   coincided   with   various   efforts   by
private   groups,   who   had   heard   of,   or   witnessed
first   hand,   the   development   of   radio   in   other
countries,   to   persuade   the   government   to   start   a
proper   radio   broadcasting   service.   The   effect   of
the   devastation   was   to   convince   officials   that   a
more   efficient   information   system   provided   by
broadcasting   would   have   averted   some   of   the
confusion   which   followed   in   the   wake.   Steps   were
therefore   taken   by   the   Ministry   of   Communications
to   organise   a   system   of   radio   broadcasting.   In   the
same   year   an   ordinance   was   established   by   the
government,   authorising   and   creating   the   supervisory
structure   for   radio   broadcasting.

The   first   Japanese   broadcasting   signals   were
transmitted   by   the   Tokyo   Broadcasting   Station   in
March 1925.   In   1926   three   temporary   stations   which
had   been   established   in   Tokyo,   Osaka   and   Nagoya
were   merged   to   form   NHK,   funded   by   fees   paid   by
listeners.   This   was   established   as   a   public
utility,   privately   managed,   under   the   close
supervision of the government. In effect the model
adopted   was   that   of   the   BBC,   a   public   service
broadcasting   organisation,   built   on   the   notion   that
radio   had   to   operate   for   the   public   good   rather
than   for   private   profit.   The   subsequent   years   saw
an   ever   increasing   domination   of   schedules   by   the
government as Japan shifted into a rabid nationalism
and   militarism.   Nevertheless,   buried   beneath   these
new   ideological   adornments   lay   the   foundations   of
public   service   which   were   to   be   continued   and
indeed   enhanced   after   1945.

From   1945   to   1950   though   NHK   continued   to
function   as   a   privately   managed   public   service
body,   it   was   under   the   close   supervision   of   the   US

198

dominated military government known by the acronym SCAP. Censorship and tight editorial control were maintained, and the organisation was purged of elements held by the occupying power to be unacceptable on grounds of attitude or past behaviour. On the 11th November 1946 a new Japanese government was promulgated, with a commitment to pacifism, a doctrine of popular sovereignty and a respect for fundamental human rights. Article 21 of the promulgation guaranteed freedom of 'speech, press and all other forms of expression'. At the same moment censorship by the military government was abolished.

On the 3rd May 1947, the new Constitution of Japan came into effect. In the months before that date SCAP instructed the communications Ministry to revise existing laws and regulations regarding broadcasting and communications so as to reflect 'the spirit' of the Constitution. In the eyes of its makers, NHK was to be many things, but it was not to be a governmental lap dog.

On the 22nd December 1949, three related Bills were published, which eventually became law on 1st June 1950 as: (i) The Radio Law, (ii) The Broadcasting Law, (iii) The Radio Regulatory Commission Establishment Law. As of that day, on which the laws came into effect, the old Nippon Hoso Kyokai juridicial body was dissolved and the new NHK established.

(i) The Radio Law
This replaced the old Wireless Telegraphy Law of 1915, becoming thereby the principal legislative enactment regulating radio communications. Its central purpose was the efficient ordering of the utilisation of radio waves.

(ii) The Broadcast Law
This stated that:

> broadcasting enterprises are subject to the regulation by the Broadcast Law in the aspects of the programming and other business matters. This is because it is necessary to regulate broadcasting so as to meet the public welfare and to strive for sound development thereof, in view of its powerful influence on our daily life.

The Law established a dual system of broadcasting, with on the one hand, NHK as the public service organisation, faced by commercial, private broadcasting organisations on the other. NHK was to be established as a corporate body in charge of public broadcasting services, responsible for its operations to the National Diet. The Broadcast Law also laid down a number of important prescriptions. It established, for example, that broadcasters,'(a) shall not disturb the public security and good morals and manners; (b) shall be politically impartial; (c) shall broadcast news without distorting facts; (d) as regards controversial issues shall clarify the points of issues from all angles possible'. The Law also laid down the basic guidelines for broadcasters' programming policies, insisting that they 'shall provide cultural programmes or educational programmes, as well as news programmes and entertainment programmes, maintaining harmony among broadcast programmes'.

The most immediately obvious feature of the Law is the extent to which it defined NHK as autonomous, neither state-owned nor commercially based, funded by a listening fee. This, in a sense, was in keeping with elements of the pre-war ideas about broadcasting. The difference in 1950 was that the public service intentions were embedded in a set of constitutional arrangements and also in the effects of a national trauma. The various articles of the Broadcast Law refer to the need to care for the public welfare (Article 1, item 1); of ensuring freedom of expression by guaranteeing the impartiality, integrity and autonomy of broadcasting (Article 1, item 2); and, by ensuring that broadcasting contributes to the development of a healthy democracy (Article 1, item 3). Even the delicate relationship between institutional autonomy, formal law and informal commitments shows some clear, even remarkable, parallels between NHK and the BBC model. This is even more remarkable given that this seems to have been the result of similar trains of thought arriving at a similar conclusion, rather than obviously imitative model building. In one respect - the legalising of commercial television broadcasts - the Broadcast Law anticipated developments in Britain.

(iii) <u>Radio Regulatory Commission Establishment Law</u>
This was modelled on the independent regulatory commission system in the United States and was empowered to regulate the emission of radio waves and generally supervise broadcasting through its quasi-legal function.

Television and Cable Policy in Japan: An Essay

In April 1951, provisional licences were granted to 10 commercial radio companies. The first television service was inaugurated by the Nippon Television Network (NTN) in August 1952, followed by NHK's first television service in February 1953. By the early 1950s the basic structure, organisation and purpose of the whole of Japanese broadcasting was thus complete. It rested on an assumed creative tension between the public service, slightly worthy NHK which was nevertheless massive, and the federal structure of aggresively commercial stations who may have done worthy things, but who were unlikely to do so and who were certainly not expected to do so.

The present structure of broadcasting and the ways in which it fits into the overall telecommunications structure can be represented schematically in Table 8.1.

Table 8.1: Telecommunications regulatory Structure

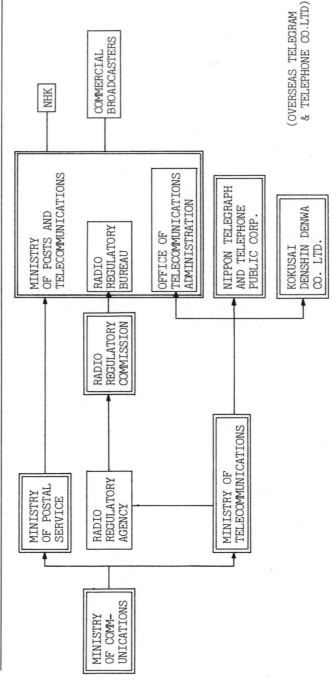

202

Television   and   Cable   Policy   in   Japan: An   Essay

The important difference in the general output of NHK compared with that of commercial television are described in Table 8.2.

Table 8.2: Programming Categories for NHK and Commercial Television

	NHK	Commercial Television
News	32.8%	11.6%
Culture	24.8%	24.9%
Entertainment	26.1%	47.1%
Education	16.3%	12.4%
Sports	-	2.8%
Other	-	1.2%

The general structure of Japanese broadcasting as at the beginning of this decade was:

NHK
2 television channels providing on one general entertainment, news, and cultural programmes and on the other, educational programmes with a high instructional content.
    2 AM radio stations, again with general entertainment, news and culture on one, and educational programming on the other.
    1 FM radio station, offering classical and popular music in 75 per cent of its output.

Commercial Television
with 97 stations, of which 36 offered TV and radio, and 61 only television.

    The actual revenues available to commercial television are considerably greater than those available to NHK. In fiscal year 1981, for example, television advertising revenue was 834 billion yen, which was 34 per cent of the total national expenditure on advertising.[1] The revenue from NHK's viewers contracts was 273 billion yen. One has, of course, to allow for the fact that NHK is a single entity whereas the advertising revenue is divided between almost a hundred different companies.
    On a national average people in Japan have

access to between 4 and 8 TV channels, 3 to 6 medium-wave radio channels, 1 to 2 FM channels and one short-wave channel. Most channels are on the air for about 17 to 22 hours a day. There are television receivers in about 99 per cent of Japan's 30 million households. Average viewing is 3 hours and 6 minutes on weekdays, 3 hours 18 minutes on Saturdays and 3 hours 46 minutes on Sundays (a pattern which shows a slight decline over the past 5 years). In short, Japan is a society in which there is almost total physical saturation of television, with a slightly declining tendency to watch. Nevertheless, TV is clearly a ubiquitous presence within Japanese culture and society.

In March 1982 however the Research and Study Council on the Diversification of Broadcasting, an advisory body to the Ministry of Posts and Telecommunications, published the results of a survey conducted in Tokyo and in Kofu in Yamanashi prefecture to the west of Tokyo. This survey showed that practically no-one living in areas which had access to five channels wanted more. Where, however, there were only two channels available people did want more. The respondents to the survey also complained about the lack of variety in programmes and wanted more music, films and news, in that order, along with more information on health, medical treatment, hobbies and learning. In October 1982, NHK also conducted a survey which examined the wishes of the Japanese public in terms of future services. On the question of whether they wanted more channels, 26.8 per cent did, 63.2 per cent wanted no more, 6.3 per cent thought there were too many already, and 3.7 per cent didn't know.

The interesting feature of this kind of finding, which has been confirmed by other surveys, is that there does not seem to exist one of the essential prerequisites of the lobby for the development of cable television, which is that the public would like to have a vastly increased choice of programme material which, in a physical sense, only broadband cable can deliver. This has probably never been the case anywhere and there is a lot of evidence from the United States that once one goes beyond, say, 12 channels the level of public interest, or certainly willingness to pay, falls off dramatically. This makes good sense, of course, since even the most passionate devotee of television would find it difficult to know what to do with 200 channels of television, always assuming that someone could find enough programming to fill the space available.

In Japan, however, the lobby for the development of cable television along lines which would be recognisable to the European or North American eye has to begin with the basic fact that the Japanese public is broadly satisfied with the television it gets and does not especially want to have a vast expansion of what is available, through cable or any other means of distribution which the wit of man might devise.

It is from within this context then that one has to place both the present condition of cable television and its likely future development. That future is tied up with the aspirations of Japan to move from a society based on the export of manufactured goods to one based on the utilisation of information - its production and distribution. Masahiro Kawahata, writing in Studies of Broadcasting in 1980, noted that Japanese economic growth was slowing down, particularly in those areas which had led its growth, steel, fabrication, assembly industries such as electrical appliances and cars. He added:

> Japan should not cling to such past glory but start seeking a new way as a trading country. There is no model for her to follow. However, Japan must find and develop new fields of industries. Under such circumstances one suggestion would be a combination of the information processing and communication technology ... the society is undergoing a transition from industry orientation to information orientedness; the centre of industry is shifting from physical production to intellectual production .

It is precisely that kind of thinking which has lain behind the development of communications policy in Japan in recent years, and it has to be said it goes a long way further than the rather narrow and poverty-stricken imagination which has so far guided related policies in Britain.

As in most other industrial societies, cable television developed in Japan simply as a means of distributing clear pictures to areas which would otherwise not receive them. Television had started in Japan in 1953 and by the end of the 1950s most urban areas were covered by signals from NHK and commercial broadcasting stations. At the same time

205

Television and Cable Policy in Japan: An Essay

however many MATV and CATV stations were established in areas where the mountainous terrain made reception extremely difficult. Most of these stations consisted of a joint reception facility established and operated by a local voluntary organisation of residents. All that one then had to do was to inform the ministry of Posts and Telecommunications that one intended to establish the facility. NHK which was anyhow obliged by law to provide a service to the whole of Japan actively assisted in advising on the construction of local cable systems, and from 1961 onwards started covering some of the costs of such developments. The net result was that during the 1960s some 5 to 6000 new cable systems were built. Cable, however, was then viewed as being no more than one more means of receiving NHK's signals and those of commercial television stations not otherwise available.

Slowly there were efforts to begin production of programmes for the cable systems. The first such attempt was in Gujo Hachiman City of Gifu Prefecture in 1963. The arrival of relay stations of the major television companies soon put an end to this local outburst of innovation and initiative. In October 1968 Nippon Cable Vision Network (NCV) started services in Shinjuku, Tokyo by linking together shops and houses whose reception had been affected by the creation of tall buildings. Its subscribers were hardly vast and numbered only 40 but the management were sufficiently ambitious to believe in the possible potential of the development of cable and were among the first to raise the idea of the wired city. As that notion began to gain currency, however, increasingly questions were asked about whether it was right and proper that under the existing law governing the development of cable all one had to do was, as it were, inform the appropriate Ministry that one was setting up a cable system and then proceed about one's daily affairs.

One had therefore the kernel of the debate about the development of cable which has continued to rage. Whether on the one hand to allow the whole thing to expand within a liberal climate and reap the alleged rewards of the services which can flow through broadband cable. Or whether one should impose controls in the interests of an orderly supervision of the existing ecology of communications.

The immediate reaction of the Ministry of Posts and Telecommunications was to impose stricter

206

controls and in 1969 a Bill was introduced into the Parliament which would have required the licensing of cable systems. A hail of criticism at what was seen as a reactionary and unnecessary measure persuaded the members of Parliament to reject the proposal. Having thus failed to get new legislation through the front door, the government tried a back door method. It proposed the establishment in each prefecture of non-profit Cable Vision Foundations and indeed in the late 1960s and early 1970s four were established in Tokyo, Kyoto-Osaka-Kobe, Nagoya and Fukuoka. The Foundations were to be made up of various participants including NHK, commercial local TV stations, newspaper publishers, the Nippon Telegraph and Telephone Corporation, power companies, electronics firms and banks. In Tokyo NCV joined the Foundation. The point was that in placing the control of cable systems within the shell of the Foundation through an administrative measure the Ministry of Posts and Telecommunications had succeeded in gaining control because under Japanese law a non-profit Foundation is obliged to obtain permission for each of its activities.

What emerged, however, was that very few viewers complained of the problem of reception because of tall buildings - the ostensible reason for establishing the Foundations being that they would ensure good reception - and even fewer were prepared to pay extra money to obtain their better pictures. In short, the new cable organisations were not inundated with would-be subscribers. Other prefectures simply did not bother to establish the Foundation. For the Ministry, it was back to the drawing board, which in effect meant back to an attempt to introduce a new law.

A Cable Television Broadcast Bill was introduced into Parliament in 1971. Criticism of the proposed legislation was once more widespread. It was said that the Bill was wrong to specify cable as supplementary to TV; that it did not come to grips with the future potential of cable, for interactivity, for example; that it was wrong to try and control the content of communications over cable; that bodies other than just the Ministry should be involved in licensing - the assumption being that those other bodies would be more liberal minded. Perhaps the most powerful opposition to the regimen of control over cable proposed by the Ministry of Posts and Telecommunications came from the increasingly powerful Trade and Industry Ministry. It wanted a liberal - or what we would

call a de-regulated - structure for cable to
enhance its telecommunications and, therefore,
economic prospects. Indeed, as a shot across the
bows of its rival, the Ministry of Trade and
Industry announced in 1971 that it was to establish
an experiment in a community of a local information
system.

In 1972, the Cable Television Broadcast Law
was passed by Parliament. It stipulated among other
things that any cable station with more than 500
terminals required a licence from the Ministry of
Posts and Telecommunications. The Minister however,
in doing so, had to consult a Cable Broadcast
Council as well as ask the opinion of the governor
of the prefecture in which the system was to be
sited. The law also stipulated that cable TV had to
be operated by a 'licensee for facilities' and an
'operator'. The former was a person(s) who built
the cable system and was obliged to retransmit any
TV signals available in his area simultaneously and
in their original form, as well as, if he so
wished, providing other original programming. The
latter was someone who would use the cable to
transmit information, or who actually rented a
channel from the licensee, and in fact the law
stipulates that the licensee must provide that
channel if he does not intend to use it.

While the principle of the law was that it was
the facility which is licensed, rather than the
enterprise, the Cable Law made it clear that the
actual content of original programmes for cable
must comply with the provisions of the Broadcast
Law which governs off-air broadcasting. The
assumption here is that while the means of
transmission may be different, there is little or
no distinction to be made between cable TV and
broadcasting, in that both are viewed in the home
where, for example, children might be present.
There was no provision within the cable legislation
for the use of cable for interactive services. In
other words, the law governing cable television
quite specifically excluded its particular use for
information purposes which presuppose the existence
of interactivity. Hence the inclusion of 'Broadcast'
in its title.

At the end of 1982 there were 3 3/4 million
homes served by cable, the vast majority of which
simply re-broadcast signals from the main
broadcasting organisations. About 89 systems with
approximately 180,000 subscribers produce their own
programmes to a limited extent - on average no more

than one hour per day. There is now an underswell of interest from commercial sources to develop cable, partly because of the long term information technology developments, but also because of the sense that a demand for more entertainment services through cable can be stimulated. For example, Toshiba has joined forces with American Television and Communications to develop cable television. Seibu Cable Vision is a joint venture between the Seibu group of railways and department stores and the National Association of Commercial Broadcasters. Their aim is to create a whole series of small cable stations serving local needs.

It was always possible that the economically liberal minded government of Mr Nakasone might look benignly on these requests to develop such cable services, along the lines of the American model which has so beguiled the leaders of many European countries. It seems certain however that such developments will remain no more than, on the one hand, a sideshow to the activities of the massive existing terrestrial broadcasters of NHK and its commercial rivals, and, on the other, to the massively ambitious information technology ambitions of both the Japanese government and the private sector. It is to telecommunications and information society policies in Japan that one really has to look for the future of cable as a communicating system.

This is necessarily a massive subject, since it entails in fact the efforts of a country which now provides one-tenth of the total global national product to transform the roots of its wealth.

From January 1976 to December 1977 the Ministry of Posts and Telecommunications had undertaken an experimental cable service at Tama New Town, West of Tokyo.Known as the Co-axial Cable Information System (CCIS), a variety of services were offered to a small number of participants. These included a retransmission service, original broadcasts, a pay-TV service, a flash information service, a facsimile newspaper, a still picture request service and so on. At Scuba City - known as Science City - in 1985 there will be a similar government sponsored interactive co-axial cable experiment in operation.

The Japanese have made considerable advances in satellite communications in recent years. In February 1983 a domestic telecommunications satellite was launched, with a back up satellite launched in August of that year. In 1984 a satellite providing direct broadcast signals was launched (BS2), carrying NHK signals to previously inaccessible areas and reaching about 400,000 homes. In 1989, there are plans for a second DBS system carrying NHK signals, but using high definition transmissions along with a third, private channel.

NTT is developing what is termed the information network system (INS). This is seen as a logical formalisation of the relationship which can exist between telecommunications and computers and which provides the infrastructure of the information society. In the words of one of the principal architects and exponents of INS, Yasusada Kitahara, it is 'the fifth stage of the evolution of communications'.[2] He states:

> ... it is necessary to digitalise the telecommunications network, and to efficiently and economically provide all kinds of communications services, including such non-telephone services as facsimile, data communications, and visual communications. It is also essential to establish a comprehensive system based on the integration of computers and digitalised telecommunications networks. This comprehensive system will integrally link digitalised telecommunications technology and computer to provide for the transmission, storage and processing of information.

It is that comprehensive system which is being developed as INS. Initial experiments in the translation of the concept into reality have been taking place in Mitaka City, a suburb of Tokyo, as well as in Kasumigaseki in Tokyo.

The Ministry of Posts and Telecommunications has its own scheme to develop 'teletopia', a series of experiments in which cable is employed to vastly increase the extent to which communities can communicate with themselves. Existing cable systems are being utilised in this scheme in which homes and local institutions are linked into a 'highly communicating society'.

Not to be outdone, the mighty MITI, the Trade and Industry Ministry, has its own established experiment at Higashi-Ikoma, the HI-OVIS experiment, an acronym meaning highly interactive visual information system. In this, a small community has been made totally interactive using optical fibre, with each household having access to a wide variety of forms of information and communications. The experiment has been underway since 1978, and while the sociological evidence seems to be highly favourable, the costs have been enormous. MITI has also announced a series of 'new media communities', planned to be in operation from 1985 to 1988 in which new local communication systems, funded by the local government and industry, will provide a range of services according to particular local needs.

What one can see then in Japan is the development of a clear sense of the new information society; the development of a number of highly advanced, well funded projects to test the social, infrastructural, economic configuration of this new socio-cultural order; and a recognition that the sea change of the information society will not just be a drifting in with the tide of entertainment, fed by superficial consumer needs to be titillated and beguiled by the frothy offerings of Hollywood and its ilk.

NOTES

1. In January 1985, the value of the Yen was as follows: 285 Yen : £1 ; 263 Yen : $1.
2. Yasusada Kitahara: Information Network System: Telecommunications in the 21st Century. Heinemann, 1984, p.10.

CONTRIBUTORS

Claude-Jean Bertrand is at the University of Paris-X (Nanterre). He has published several books on the media, including The British Press and Les Medias aux Etats-Units, and has recently edited (jointly with Francis Bordat) an issue of Trimedia devoted to cable television in the United States. He is currently editing a book on World Media.

Kees Brants has written extensively on the media and is currently at the Institute of Political Science at the University of Amsterdam.

Geoffrey Caldwell is Senior Lecturer at the Centre for Continuing Education at the Australian National University, Canberra.

André H. Caron is an Associate Professor at the Department of Communication, University of Montréal, Canada. His research interest includes the cultural impact of the American media, particularly cable, on Canada.

Rolf-Rüdiger Hoffman works for a housing association in Hamburg and occasionally teaches at Hamburg University.

Nick Jankowski is at the Institute of Mass Communication Studies, The Catholic University, Nijmegen, The Netherlands. He has written extensively on community television.

Ralph Negrine is Senior Lecturer at the City of London Polytechnic, London. His research interests include the new technologies and community media.

Michael Schacht has worked for several media organisations in Germany. He is now the editor of 'Kabel und Satellit. Die Neue Mediamarketen'. He has also researched into the whole question of local and community television.

Vernone Sparkes is Associate Professor at the S.I. Newhouse School of Public Communication, Syracuse University, New York. He has written on aspects of municipal and state regulations as well as community programming.

CONTRIBUTORS

James R. Taylor is Professor at the Department of
Communication, University of Montréal. He was
recently also appointed special adviser to the
Deputy Prime Minister at the Department of
Communication in Ottawa.

Michael Tracey is head of the Broadcasting Research
Unit at the British Film Institute. He is the
author of many books on broadcasting including The
Production of Political Television, Whitehouse and
A Variety of Lives: a biography of Hugh Greene.

GLOSSARY

BROADBAND: a general term used to describe a communication system which carries a wide frequency range so allowing for a wide range of simultaneous transmissions, e.g. cable TV, satellite and so on.

CATV: community antenna television systems usually serving entire towns or major suburbs.

CO-AXIAL CABLE: a term which refers to the copper co-axial cable which is the most common type of cable used in cable systems. Such a cable system usually requires a series of amplifiers at regular intervals to boost the signal. See also FIBRE-OPTIC CABLE (below).

COMMON CARRIER: an organisation which operates a communications service, e.g. telephones, available to the public at standard rates. The carrier has no control over content.

DBS: Direct Broadcasting by Satellite: a geostationary satellite which broadcasts signals of sufficient power that they can be picked up by domestic receivers.

FIBRE-OPTIC CABLE: a cable system which uses long, very thin glass fibres which can transmit light signals with very little distortion. These signals can be modulated to carry many forms of information such as TV signals and data.

INTERACTIVE: a cable system's ability to carry signals from the head-end to the subscriber or other points in the networks and vice versa. In some systems, subscribers may be able to send back simple instructions or information, e.g. for shopping or expressing a voting preference.

LPTV: LOW POWER TV: satellite transmissions which are of a lower power than those of DBS and can only be picked up by large non-domestic antenna.

MATV-MASTER ANTENNA TV: a cable system which provides a service to dwellings within an individual building such as a block of flats or housing estates.

GLOSSARY

MDS-MULTI-POINT DISTRIBUTION SYSTEM: a system which distributes its television signals by their transmission at microwave frequencies to subscribers. See also STV (below).

MSO-MULTIPLE SYSTEM OPERATOR: refers to the concentration, e.g. of ownership, within the industry.

PTT: refers to the national and usually publicly owned postal, telephone and telegraph companies of such countries as France and Germany. Britain recently returned to private ownership British Telecom, the national telecommunications company.

SMATV-SATELLITE MASTER ANTENNA TV: usually refers to a system which serves dwellings within individual buildings such as a block of flats.

STV-SUBSCRIPTION TV: off-air subscription TV using available UHF frequencies to supply one or two channels to large markets. The signals are usually scrambled.

TELETEX: a method of transmitting information using television broadcast transmissions. It is a one-way system which does not allow the user to send commands back. See VIDEOTEX (below).

VCR: VIDEO CASSETTE RECORDER.

VIDEOTEX: name used to describe any electronic system which makes computer based information available either through visual display units (VDUs) or specially adapted television sets. There are two main types: broadcast videotex (in Britain called Ceefax or Oracle) and wired videotex (in Britain the main one is known as Prestel) which allows the user to access computer based information via public telephone lines and at the user's command.

INDEX

Index

Index